THE CASE FOR ASLAN

The Case for Aslan

Evidence for Jesus in the Land of Narnia

David Marshall

To Bob and Elaine Colvin

for books borrowed, and books you helped me write

Contents:

Introduction 7

1. Puddleglum's Wager: Is Narnia just a Dream? 16

2. The Lion's Song (Creation) 33

3. Turkish Delight (Temptation) 53

4. Interview with Aslan (Incarnation. 68

5. Susan Comes Calling (Gospel Truth) 87

6. A Different Sort of Magic (Miracles) 106

7. The Witch's Revenge (Crucifixion) 125

8. Deeper Magic (Resurrection) 138

9. Into Aslan's Shadow (Judgement) 153

10. Tash vs. Aslan (Other Religions) 166

11. Canceling Aslan (Justice) 187

12. Imagining Truth 207

Introduction

I stepped off the bus from Heathrow onto High Street and caught my first glimpse of Oxford's famous "dreaming spires." The limestone towers of this city (along with pillars in Athens, olives of Mount Zion, and cedars beneath Mount Tai in the State of Lu) have, one could say, dreamed much of the world into being. A few paces up High Street hung a plaque to Robert Boyle, one of the founders of modern chemistry, and Robert Hooke, who studied cork under a microscope, and discovered what he called the "cell." Behind that wall rose the turrets of University College, one of Oxford's oldest schools. In its cells studied, among others, Bill Clinton, Stephen Hawking, and the poet Percy Shelley. As a student, Shelley wrote a tract called "The Necessity of Atheism," sending a copy to all the bishops and college heads, and getting kicked out of the university. Across the street rose one of the city's oldest and loveliest spires: St. Mary's Cathedral, where a former University College student and skeptic named Jack Lewis who now found atheism unnecessary, offered hope in the midst of World War II:

> We discern the freshness and purity of morning, but they do not make us fresh and pure. We cannot mingle with the splendors we see. But all the leaves of the New Testament are rustling with the rumor that it will not always be so. Some day, God willing, we shall get *in*.

Do stones dream? ("Further up and further in!") Might their souls come alive at night?

Another Oxford graduate, the fantasy writer Philip Pullman, once suggested that the gargoyles of New and Magdalene Colleges descend from their perches after dusk to do battle.

Oxford's humans certainly have mixed it up. At Balliol, John Wycliffe translated the Bible into English. During a quarrel between Catholics and Protestants over how to read that book, three martyrs (or heretics, if you will) were tried at St. Mary's, then "lit a fire as shall never be put out" on Broad Street. Bishop Wilberforce and Thomas Huxley debated evolution among old bones at the university museum. After inventing chemistry, Boyle willed a series of lectures defending the Christian faith against the likes of Shelley, Pullman, and Huxley. Three future reformers studied at Christ Church: John Wesley, John Locke, and William Penn. Their Christian visions merged in Philadelphia (in a colony named for Penn's father) to help form the United States of America. After leaving Oxford, Shelley wrote an anti-God poem, *Prometheus Unbound*, that inspired Karl Marx with a dream of revolution that would form the Warsaw Pact, which would point nuclear-laden ICBMs at democratic towns.

Boyle's Law and Hooke's cell were not the only cutting-edge scientific concepts to emerge from this community. Here, Roger Bacon fractured light and described its nature. Here, the Merton Calculators explained how geometry could describe motion. At Wadham College, John Wilkins gathered friends, including Boyle and Hooke, who became the Royal Society, the world's oldest and most influential scientific club. These stones briefly hosted Erwin Schrodinger, with his quantum equations and cat of Cheshire-like indeterminacy. (Charles Dodgson, who made the vanishing smile of the Cheshire cat famous, taught math at Christ Church.) Here, Edward Tylor explained how religion began, until his student Andrew Lang discovered primitive monotheism and debunked

Tylor's "animistic" theory. Here, too, James Legge introduced the Chinese Classics to the western world.

Yet Oxford's literary daydreams inspire us even more deeply. A girl chases a white rabbit. A hobbit puts a golden ring in his pocket. Another girl sets out to find dust and save all worlds from an evil, heretic-hunting Magisterium. Scenes for stories about a school for witches were filmed or imagined here. Children meet a talking lion.

Perhaps we need such "escapes" in part, because our universities, where diverse curiosities once met in a vision of God, have lost their universality. Society fractured into tribes again. Mind has been divorced from heart. Our dreaming spires seem to have lost their deepest inspiration. As historian of Chinese philosophy, Feng Yulan, put it, "That which can be believed, cannot be loved. And that which can be loved, cannot be believed."

That's how Jack Lewis felt when he returned to Oxford from the front lines in France, with their "horribly smashed men still moving like half-crushed beetles, the sitting or standing corpses, the landscape of sheer earth without a blade of grass." He was deeply moved by the mythologies of the Greeks, Irishs, and Norse, as if hearing a call from another world. But he doubted any Voice could give that call: "Nearly all that I loved I believed to be imaginary: nearly all that I believed to be real, I thought grim and meaningless."

Lewis took first-class degrees in English, Greek and Latin Literature, and Philosophy and Ancient History, and began to teach philosophy. A few years later, however, he wrote a book subtitled "An Allegorical Apology for Christianity, Reason and Romanticism." Jack Lewis had found what looked like a solution. He had met Someone he could both believe, and love.

Jack the Giant-Killer

Lewis' ideas gained a hearing. He defended his Christian faith not only in churches, but to large audiences on the BBC, and in popular books. *Time Magazine* featured him on its front cover. *National Review* rated his *Mere Christianity* and *Abolition of Man* as the best and eighth-best non-fiction books of the 20th Century. One could find copies of Lewis' non-fiction under the night lamps of Francis Collins, who led the Human Genome Project, and of Pope John Paul II. Into the 21st Century, in his *God Delusion*, Richard Dawkins, the most famous atheist in the world (and a New College gargoyle) came down to attack that old Madeleine College grotesque, and his "ludicrously inadequate" arguments for the Christian faith.

But the ideas in Lewis' "serious" books proved magical in their own way, like the wings of a butterfly that stir up a typhoon on the other side of the world.

Charles Colson was known as Richard Nixon's "hatchet man." He had served as a Marine and become a hard-driving lawyer, ruthlessly cutting corners to "get things done" for his boss, the president of the United States. But as often happens to trolls, apes, and shepherd-boys who lie in fairy tales, Colson was trapped by his own "dirty tricks." He fell from power and was headed to prison. A friend lent him a copy of *Mere Christianity*. Colson found Lewis' arguments convincing, and was "born again," as his best-selling autobiography was titled.

A Filipino senator named Benigno Aquino was imprisoned by the dictator Ferdinand Marcos. He read Colson's book and experienced a spiritual awakening. Aquino was allowed to fly to America for bypass surgery. Seven years later, he returned, hoping to talk Marcos into allowing the Philippines more freedom. "The Filipino is worth dying for," he boldly declared.

Aquino was gunned down at the airport. Led by Catholic bishops, a respected general, and Aquino's widow, two million Filipinos gathered and asked Marcos to go away.

When he did, copy-cat People Power movements broke out in Burma, Eastern Europe, and China. The Berlin Wall fell and was sold in chunks as stocking stuffers at Christmas, 1989. One could thus argue that Lewis' "ludicrously inadequate" arguments did at least help melt Soviet ice and bring Father Christmas back to Red Square.

So why did a man known for erudite works of literary scholarship, satirical science fiction, and such popular defenses of the faith, who had no children, suddenly start writing about talking lions and dancing fauns? And why have those stories sold some 100 million copies? Did Lewis lose confidence in the intellectual power of the Gospel? Were the skeptics winning the Battle of Gremlins? Had his efforts to shore up the ancient spires of Christian faith, eaten away by the acid of doubt, come to naught? Was the great Christian scholar seeking a safe space from dangerous skeptical ideas by returning to childhood fancies?

Aslan comes to Oxford

On February 2, 1948, at a small college on the banks of the Cherwell, where Lewis Carroll once took a girl named Alice punting, C. S. Lewis defended his favorite argument for God in debate with the Catholic philosopher, Elizabeth Anscombe.

Lewis' most famous biographer, A.N. Wilson, says he was trounced and "stung back into childhood by his defeat." Lewis gave up defending the Christian faith rationally, Wilson argued, and retreated to childhood fancies. And that (said Wilson) is how Aslan was born.

An ill-omened birth, others complain. Fantasy writer Allan Garner, who studied literature at Magdalen while Lewis was still there, described the Narnia books as "nasty, manipulative, morbid, misanthropic, hectoring, totalitarian and atrociously written." Philip Pullman called them "ugly" and "poisonous." He accused Lewis of sexism, racism, and a "sado-masochistic" flair for violence. He complained that Lewis damned his heroine, Susan, to hell for wanting to grow up. J. K. Rowling also complained about Lewis' treatment of Susan. Even J. R. R. Tolkien, who credited his friend for encouraging him to write the *Lord of the Rings*, expressed artistic doubts about Narnia.

I will argue that Narnia is neither escapist nor morally repulsive, but is a brilliant artistic and intellectual success. Aslan speaks truth to our minds as well as our hearts. *The Chronicles of Narnia* show why by another name, he can be both believed and loved. Jack Lewis' "childish" dream reconciles human experience, making the university of ideas universal again: quantum theory and Medieval philosophy, the Big Bang and "In the Beginning," justice and disgust over Cancel Culture, faith and reason, familiar old stories and new insights into human nature.

The Gifts of Father Christmas

The best moment in the first Narnia film comes when Lucy walks through the wardrobe door, and watches with shiny eyes as snow falls in a quiet forest lit by a lone lamp. One of the privileges of being "Dad" or "Mom" is the chance to watch that same light appear in the faces of our children as they crawl towards a spot of sunshine on the linoleum, laugh at a bushy-tailed squirrel running up a fir, or stand along a cold lakeshore in Southeast Alaska, the "dreaming spires" of mountain peaks rising all around, grab a chunk of hard glacial ice, and naively ask (as my son did), "Is this the North Pole?"

Narnia calls us to wonder. Digory Kirke was "the sort of person who wants to know everything." Caspian the Seafarer sailed to the end of the world. At the threshold of the Land of Bism, Prince Rilian spoke as the anti-Hamlet, pulled by dueling desires, rather than despairs: "It may be no mortal man has ever looked into Bism before or will ever have the chance again. And I know not how, as the years pass, I shall bear to remember that it was once in my power to have probed the uttermost pit of Earth and that I forebore."

Explorers in our world have also been busy since Reepicheep pointed the bow of his kayak into the "greenish-grey, trembling, shimmering" wall of water at the end of the world. The screen in your pocket holds pixelized images of a galaxy of imagined realities, and vastly more information than all the books in the Bodleian library. We probe elementary particles and galaxies so distant they still glow with the light of Creation. We study left-handed amino acids, continents that once covered the earth, and habitable zones around exoplanets. We dust off Clovis spear-tips at campsites in New Mexico, or monoliths at Pot Belly Hill in Turkey, where early man built some of his first temples. Solutions to the problem of the Historical Jesus grace the covers of leading magazines. China and India reemerge as giants. A tall mosque now rises a short walk from Magdalene College, while the Institute for Hindu Studies meets a few doors down from the Eagle and Child pub.

What does Silicon Valley have to do with Cair Paravel? Aslan with Osama? Marshwiggles with mutations in the protein spikes of Wuhan coronaviruses?

C. S. Lewis did not "retreat" into Narnia. His coracle still leads to Aslan's Country, where one finds truths "alive and growing" like rubies in the land of Bism, capable of changing our world.

Father Christmas gave gifts to children who visited Narnia: a sword, a shield, medicine made from flowers in the sun, bow and arrows, a horn that would bring aid when blown.

Narnia still offers many gifts. Among them is a juice made from flowers of the Son, which heals the fatal divide between myth and reality, faith and reason, science and literature, and lets gargoyles dream happy dreams that may come true.

Puddleglum, who has cured gnomes of gloomy bewitchments before, will be our first guide to philosophy, as we first seek to understand how faith and reason can be reconciled.

Suggested Reading

Beginning: You can enter Narnia through one of two portals: the wardrobe door Lucy found in *The Lion, the Witch, and the Wardrobe*, which introduces these stories in the order in which they were written, or *The Magicians Nephew*, where you can watch the world made in Narnia's own time. But before turning the next page, please read *The Silver Chair*. There you will meet a seminal figure in the history of philosophy who also cooks a mean eel soup.

Advanced: Many have rightly criticized A. N. Wilson's biography of C. S. Lewis for its inaccuracies. But Wilson is wonderful writer, and his version of the Lewis story is worth reading. The best account of Lewis' life, though, is by his good friend George Sayer.

Grad-Level: Walter Hooper did C. S. Lewis fans a wonderful service by carefully editing and annotating Lewis' letters in three volumes that total some 3400 pages. While Lewis hated writing letters, especially to the strangers who often pestered him, he saw it as his duty to help those who sought him out. (Even financially.) He also carried on lively correspondence with dozens of remarkable thinkers, some of whom will be mentioned later. While a few of Lewis' surviving letters are repetitious, many are brilliantly entertaining and insightful.

They also provide a kind of bibliographical sound track to Lewis' life, and an excellent "cheat sheet" for young people looking for books to furnish the living rooms of their minds.

Also mentioned in the introduction: Feng Yulan's *Short Introduction to Chinese Philosophy*. On Dawkins, see his *The God Delusion*, or my *The Truth Behind the New Atheism*.

ONE

Puddleglum's Wager

Is Narnia just a Dream?

"Narnia? Narnia? I have often heard your lordship utter that name in your ravings. Dear Prince, you are very sick. There is no land called Narnia."

"Yes there is, though, Ma'am. You see, I happen to have lived there all my life."

Two children from another world are tasked to liberate a captive Prince Caspian. They are guided north by a marshwiggle: a tall, thin biped who lives in tidal flats, enjoys eel soup for dinner, smokes mud in his pipe, "takes a sober view of life," and looks as if a lazy princess blew him half a kiss, leaving his transformation from frog to man incomplete. The three travel through Underworld, inhabited by gnomes who seldom speak and never smile, to the palace of an evil queen. There they break the spell that binds the prince.

The queen turns up, and is startled to find her erstwhile prisoner in his right mind and accompanied by friends. Seeing the tool of Rilian's enslavement destroyed (a silver chair), the lady throws hallucinogenic substances on the fire and begins to strum an "instrument like a mandolin." Then a debate on epistemology, the proper "theory of knowledge," that is what we should believe and why, breaks out.

The propriety of trust is a common question in Narnia. Does Lucy tell lies? Why not sample the candy the nice lady on the sleigh is offering? Should we follow that robin? Can one believe lions? Do other worlds really wait "just around the corner?"

Faith and reason, which together constitute the foundation of all knowledge, are among the most misunderstood Christian ideas. Puddleglum explains the intellectual magic between these two, breaking us out of the dungeon of muddled thinking that imprisons our badly confused world.

The Emerald Witch claims that her dark realm is the only reality. There is no sun. Spotting a lamp, her silly guests had just imagined a big lamp hanging in the sky and giving light to all. "Hanging from what?" she trills. Aslan the lion is just a "copy-cat," a mental projection of one of her own, smaller felines. "You can put nothing into your make-believe world without copying it from the real world of mine, which is the only world," she explains.

The queen offers three arguments, along with music and drugs, to persuade her debate partners that Narnia is a delusion. First, the country does not fit into reality as she portrays it. How can there be a nation among the rafters? Second, she offers her own testimony to deny the children's claim to have met her in Overworld. "I cry you mercy, little brother," she says with a lovely laugh, "I have no memory of that meeting." She also proposes a theory to explain their error: "We often meet our friends in strange places when we dream."

The four travelers are almost persuaded. Then Puddleglum stamps on the enchanted fire with his bare feet, and echoing the French philosopher Blaise Pascal, explains why he plans to "gamble on Aslan:"

All you've been saying is quite right, I shouldn't wonder. I'm a chap who always likes to know the worst and then put the best face I can on it. But there's one thing...

Suppose we have only dreamed, or made up, all those things— trees and grass and sun and moon and stars and Aslan himself. Suppose we have. Then all I can say is, in that case, the made-up things seem a good deal more important than the real ones. Suppose this black pit of a kingdom of yours is the only world. Well, it strikes me as a pretty poor one. And that's a funny thing, when you come to think of.

Late in 1947, Lewis had published a book called *Miracles: A Preliminary Study*, in which he argued that materialism doesn't make sense. Materialism implies that our minds are the product of irrational evolutionary forces. He cited *Possible Worlds*, by the Marxist geneticist John Haldane, to make his point: "If my mental processes are determined wholly by the motions of atoms in my brain, I have no reason to suppose that my beliefs are true... and hence I have no reason for supposing my brain to be composed of atoms."

A few months later, Lewis debated the young Catholic philosopher Elizabeth Anscombe at the Socratic Club, a student organization of which he was president. A. N. Wilson argued that Lewis lost that debate, and came to doubt that he could defend Christianity by reason. Wilson read Puddleglum's speech as Lewis' white flag of surrender: "The wounded Christian, unable to think out his position but determined, in a moving and dogged way, to be loyal to it."

Lewis retreated, Wilson claims, into a second childhood. Imagination would be the door into the Kingdom of God: giants and witches, lions singing worlds into being, children sailing to the end of the world.

In fact, Puddleglum shows remarkable clarity of thought for a marshwiggle in such a fix. No wonder! Lewis knew the queen's voice well. He had once been trapped in that pit of a kingdom called "materialism" or "determinism" himself. And not him alone.

C. S. Lewis in Underworld

Shortly after his conversion, Lewis wrote a book called *Pilgrim's Regress* that recounted his story of escape. The hero of the book, a traveler named John, had been told since youth that the Landlord (God) maintained a dark pit in the mountains filled with snakes and scorpions "as big as lobsters," and would throw anyone who broke any of a long list of rules into it. Terrified, John fled his homeland of Puritania in the opposite direction, in search of a romantic island of paradise that he sometimes glimpsed from afar.

Early on his way, John met people who denied that any such person as the Landlord existed, and gladly embraced their view. No more black pits! (A school friend described the teenage Lewis as an extremely witty and "foul-mouthed" atheist.) John then encountered a giant, whose slaves threw him into a pit with other prisoners. Whenever the giant looked into the dungeon, its eyes rendered the prisoners translucent. So if John looked at a woman, he saw her lungs, or her intestines writhing like snakes. An old man's cancer was plainly visible. The prisoners drew back from one another in horror.

"I am in the black hole!" John shouted. Maybe there was no God, but this vision of life—existence reduced to mere mechanics, "seeing through" love and thought until our humanity itself disappeared into a mass of horrors—was hellish enough.

The Lady of the Green Kirtle has the same effect on her prisoners. A lion becomes just a cat wearing a wig. The sun is merely the thermonuclear reaction of pressurized hydrogen after a large mass has swept a region of space and formed a gravity sump. Eros is evolution's way of tricking you into perpetuating the species.

Friendship is mutual back-scratching so social animals can hunt mammoths, code software, or stock shelves cooperatively. Religion is psychology, poetry is marks on paper, love is instinct, thought the firing of neurons, and politics is power. Thus citizens of every realm become slaves whose lives and even thoughts are determined by Fate.

Lewis had a name for the shrinking of thought down to motive. He called it "Bulverism," after the mythical Ezekiel Bulver, its inventor. After hearing his mother argue with his father by saying, "You just say that because you're a man," Bulver realized that evidence was not required to win debates: simply question the other person's motives. "Assume that your opponent is wrong, and explain his error, and the world will be at your feet."

The most popular forms of Bulverism in Lewis' youth were Marxism and Freudianism. The man who tossed John into the pit was named Sigismund Enlightenment, after Freud. But Bulverism has also become a pillar of modern identity politics. "You just say that because you're white." And, copying Bulver's mother, "You just say that because you're a man."

The witch's plan was to conquer Narnia and make Rilian titular king of that land (which he was due to inherit, originally.) Under the rule of her puppet, Narnia would negate itself: fauns would stop dancing, and centaurs would recognize the stars as mere photon-emitting heat sources. So the witch's claim, while bad as geography (within that world), would have become true as prophecy. Under the cloud spewing from the fire of her reductionism, Narnia would turn into Mordor. There truly would be no Narnia, anymore. *The Abolition of Man* warned of the same fate for our world.

Fortunately, the marshwiggle won. Not only did Puddleglum best the Emerald Queen in debate, he also defeated a panoply of famous human thinkers: Freud, Marx, and Haldane's successor

Richard Dawkins, along the way. He helped straighten out the tangle the modern world has made of faith and reason, not only showing why Christian hope is reasonable, but pointing the way out of our Underworld.

Puddleglum's Philosophy

The end of philosophy is to clear our heads. Three thinkers whose names all happen to start with "p" help us think clearly about faith and reason: Plato, Pascal, and Plantinga. Add Puddleglum to that number.

The famous marshwiggle called himself "a chap who always like to know the worst and then put the best face I can on it." Prince Rilian sometimes played straight man to Puddleglum's Rodney ("I get no respect") Dangerfield:

(A) Rilian: Hast hit it, friend wiggle. When our swords hacked off the Witch's head, that stroke ended all her magic works, and now the Deep Lands are falling to pieces. We are looking at the end of the Underworld.

Puddleglum: That's it, Sir. Unless it should also happen to be the end of the whole world.

(B) Rilian: This is the greatest shame and sorrow that could have fallen on us. We have sent a brave lady into the hands of enemies and stayed behind in safety.

Puddleglum: Don't paint it too black, Sir. We're not very safe except for death by starvation in this hole."

Clearly, Puddleglum is no Pangloss, the starry-eyed court thinker in Voltaire's *Candide*, who supposes that God is in His heaven and all is right with the world. Puddleglum is a rainy-day logician. He is a philosopher of the Underground, of the Dark Night of the Soul, of "the Cave," into which Plato said we are all born.

In *The Inferno*, Virgil guided Dante through the Underworld. In C. S. Lewis' *Great Divorce*, George MacDonald served as Lewis' guide to Heaven. Puddleglum will help guide our approach to Narnia, and to thinking about faith and reason in the 21st Century. For Narnia is no retreat into childhood. It is a virtual reality, a medium in which Lewis creates an experimental world and discovers truth with deep implications for our lives. Narnia is a controlled environment in which ideas about faith and reason, life and death, miracles and sin, are isolated, nurtured, observed, and tested under critical conditions.

Plato's Petri Dish

Philosophers and scientists often invent imaginary worlds to make points about this one. To illustrate the paradoxes of quantum physics, a German physicist named Erwin Schrodinger, with whom Lewis probably dined when he lived at Magdalen College in 1933, told a story about a cat in a box. The box was so constructed that the cat would die if a single radioactive particle decayed. Later we will meet Richard Lenski, who has been observing the evolution of E. coli bacteria in flasks since 1988. Writers also create worlds of thought, isolate characters within them, lend them an environment, then watch (often in surprise) how they react.

In *The Republic*, Plato created a petri dish of the imagination by telling a story about a cave. From childhood, he said, prisoners in that cave were chained neck and wrist, and forced to face in one direction. A fire burned at their backs. Men carried objects in front of the fire, the shadows of which projected on the wall in front of the prisoners. That is what life is like, Plato argued. All we see are shadows: cats not lions, lamps not sun. But suppose one of those slaves were to escape to "Overworld?" When his eyes adjusted, a far richer landscape would shock them, full of objects of which he had only held the dimmest notion. If he reentered the cave, he would not find it easy to convince other prisoners of that greater world.

Or suppose we are trapped not in a cave, but in a computer simulation? A movie called *The Matrix* famously put a technological spin on the same plot. Morpheus played a role similar to that of Puddleglum or Plato, while Neo played a skeptic unsure whether or not to believe in Overworld (though directions were reversed, in his case):

> Morpheus: The Matrix is everywhere. It is all around us. Even now, in this very room. You can see it when you look out your window or when you turn on your television. You can feel it when you go to work...when you go to church... when you pay your taxes. It is the world that has been pulled over your eyes to blind you from the truth.
>
> Neo: What truth?
>
> Morpheus: That you are a slave, Neo. Like everyone else you were born into bondage. Into a prison that you cannot taste or see or touch. A prison for your mind.

The Matrix was different from Plato's (or the witch's) Cave in one sense: the world into which Neo escaped turned out to be more hellish than that from which he fled. It had been blasted by a nuclear war. It lacked trees, flowers, sky, or good food. In fact, it was more like Underworld than Narnia. But otherwise, the question for Neo, Plato's slaves, Puddleglum, and ourselves, is the same: how do we know what is real?

Three possible sources of information are mentioned in Morpheus' dialogue: "your mind," our senses ("taste or see or touch," "look out the window," "feel,"), and other people ("when you turn on your television," "go to work," "go to church," "pay taxes"). Another source of potential knowledge is implicit: Morpheus himself, a voice from outside the petri dish, one who has traveled in Overworld or left Plato's cave and returned.

Those are the only four possible ways of realizing any fact.

Knowledge depends first on our brains. Can we trust them? Your thinking will grow dim, Aslan warned, as you descend into the low countries. Puddleglum drank giant liquor and his speech began to slur. Perhaps his memories of Overworld were just drunken illusions. Or maybe they were, as the witch said, only a dream. (Morpheus is the god of dreams.) Could he trust his tottering memory of that favorite eel hole back home? Even fawns and dwarves thought Jill mad when she started yammering about Prince Rilian and horses under the hill.

We drink, dream, even hallucinate. And if our minds, Lewis argued, are the product of blind causes, how can we be sure they ever tell the truth? Alvin Plantinga developed that question into what he calls the "Evolutionary Argument Against Naturalism." I am not entirely convinced by Plantinga's argument. If evolution can create novel organs at all (a big "if," more on that later), then it seems to me the most adaptive and simple eye to form would be one that sees things more or less as they are, and the most adaptive and simple brain would do the same. But Plantinga offered a valid warning against naïve skepticism. Even Darwin admitted to a "horrible doubt" whether human beliefs "are of any value," if our brains evolved from those of lower animals. I am often amazed at how confident many who believe their brains were formed by lucky chances, can be of their opinions. We should not dismiss our memories, beliefs, biases, and motivations (what then does the dismissing?) but "to err is human."

Secondly, can we trust our senses? Are those South Pacific fronds between the doorframe, or is the lion (or programmers in Silicon Valley) creating hallucinogenic images? Am I drinking wine, or water at a trough mixed with donkey spit? Is that a lion on the hill, or an ass wearing a skin on its back? Is the pale light in the tunnel above really the moon? A poisonous glow from a dank toadstool? An oncoming train?

Seeing is not always believing, let alone trusting. All the data from our senses comes through electric impulses channeled down nerves to brains. Why believe those impressions? Maybe the early morning scene that confronts my senses now— sun on pear blossoms, a chicken crowing a block away, a mug of hot chocolate warming my fingers and palate— is fed into my brain by a programmer. Anyway, my eyes are not what they used to be.

Yet without faith in our senses, not only can we not find our way out of Underworld, we cannot tie our shoelaces or answer a text message.

Third, can we trust government (taxes), the Media (TV) or colleagues (work)? Should one look a talking horse in the mouth when he says, "Narnia and the North?" Fleeing a powerful empire is not a step to take lightly. Will Aravis wait for me, or should I grab a watermelon and cross the desert alone? Is Eustace pulling my leg about asking what's-his-name to help us escape bullies? What happens if I grab that pretty ring?

By faith in mind, senses, and people, one gets out of bed in the morning, puts on socks and shoes, calls tech support, or checks the cloud cover before taxing down the runway. We can't live without these kinds of faith. But all three err, and must be tested by evidence. That is a reasonable circularity: without provisional and critical faith in this trinity of oracles, we can know no more than an oyster. Even a community of wolves or bees is doomed without mutual trust.

Faith, in the Christian sense, means nothing mystical or weird, but simply this: to trust and act upon what you have good reason to believe, even when fire bites or witches shriek.

The fourth level of faith is in One who claims to have traveled to Overworld, Zion, the Kingdom of Heaven. Or is life just a random dance of atoms, which scatter in the heat death of the universe and the grave?

Narnia actually is a dream. An English professor invented it in his "Spare Time." (Sister city to the equally imaginary Spare Oom, which Tumnus the faun never heard of in geography class, because it wasn't on the map.)

In his 1976 book, *The Selfish Gene*, a fellow of New College to the left looking out C. S. Lewis' office window, described religious faith as "a kind of mental illness." Thirty years later Richard Dawkins launched the New Atheism movement by publishing *The God Delusion*. In it, he claimed that Christians believe "not only in the absence of evidence, but in the teeth of evidence."

Alister McGrath wrote the first response to the movement begun by Dawkins, *Dawkin's God*, and I wrote the second, *The Truth Behind the New Atheism*. Both of us argued that Christian thinkers do not recommend "blind faith" at all. In a later anthology, *True Reason*, philosopher Tim McGrew and I defined the traditional Christian view of faith as "trusting, holding to, and acting on what one has good reason to believe is true, in the face of difficulties." (Like the spells of witches.) We showed that Christian thinkers from the Bible on have demanded that faith be grounded in facts and clear thinking. Self-professed apostles of reason have consistently ignored actual Christian thought about faith, "in the teeth of evidence." (Or tossed out half-digested references to "Doubting Thomas," Tertullian, Martin Luther, or "Pascal's Wager:" see below!) Such a lackadaisical approach will not do. Like all objects worthy of serious study, the Christian tradition must be read fairly and widely. Like McGrath, McGrew and myself, Puddleglum's creator understood the Christian idea of faith better than its modern critics.

For Christians, faith can be either "good" nor "bad." One should mistrust ladies who turn into green snakes, uncles who dabble in black magic, or giants who get you drunk. Lewis said that if you think the evidence is against Christianity, do not believe it.

Pascal and Puddleglum's Wager

The great mathematician and scientist Blaise Pascal began writing a work of apologetics in his late thirties. He died young, however, and did not complete it. What remains is a list of 923 sayings. Some are small, beautiful and finely-sculpted as jewels. Others come to us as paragraphs of prose, or like mere grocery lists of ideas stuck to the refrigerator door. All in all, *Pensees* is a brilliant, but incomplete work. We don't know exactly how Pascal planned to put all his thoughts together.

The most famous and misunderstood argument in those notes is called "Pascal's Wager."

Suppose you are unsure that God exists. Should you stay in Underworld, or seek Aslan's Country? Your choice of paths is a gamble. Bet on God, and you may forfeit some worldly pleasures. But the Kingdom of Heaven is so much greater than this world, that as Puddleglum said, it is "small loss" to invest your life in seeking it.

The Pascal-Puddleglum Wager is misunderstood in two ways. First, we forget that both philosophers are speaking to a man in a haze. We are enchanted by the smoke of desire and throbbing mandolin beat of denial. We must stomp on the fire of temptation, subjectivity and self-delusion to clear our heads.

As a scientist and mathematician, Pascal thought that more than any slave obeys his master, we should obey Reason, "for in disobeying the one we are unfortunate, and in disobeying the other we are fools." Indeed, thought "constitutes the greatness of man." Dawkins, like many modern Darwinists, is embarrassed to place man at the apex of the tree of evolution. Pascal argued that not vanity, but the inherent glory of reason forces us to recognize human nobility as the pinnacle of worldly creation.

Yet Pascal also recognized the contingent and fallible nature of our thought processes: we are but "thinking reeds." Indeed (Pascal helped invent the computer, and here he anticipated *The Matrix*), we cannot even say for sure whether we wake or sleep! "What a chimera then is man! What a novelty! What a monster, what a chaos, what a contradiction, what a prodigy! Judge of all things, imbecile worm of the earth; depositary of truth, a sink of uncertainty and error; the pride and refuse of the universe!"

"Is there no means of seeing the face of the cards?" Pascal imagined a skeptic asking. To which he replied, "Scripture and the rest." But Pascal's skeptical dialogue partner, like Prince Rilian while still bound to the silver chair, was physically restrained: "I have my hands tied and my mouth closed; I am forced to wager, and am not free."

Later chapters in *Pensees* do what skeptics deny Pascal does: rationally support the Christian faith. He offers four kinds of evidence for Christianity: miracles, prophecies, the character of Jesus, and the accounts of his life called the gospels. "I see many contradictory religions...But I see that Christian religion wherein prophecies are fulfilled." "The apostles were either deceived or deceivers. Either supposition has difficulties; for it is not possible to mistake a man raised from the dead."

You may ask if Pascal's arguments are any good. They are works in progress, with flashes of brilliance. Other Christians (including myself) have offered detailed supporting arguments in these areas, some of which we shall touch on later. But the point for now is, anyone who claims Pascal asked us to believe for no reason, is grossly misrepresenting a great thinker, and is himself ignoring the facts.

Pascal knew we need evidence, but also recognized that the heart "has its reasons, of which reason knows nothing." Aslan allows us into confusing situations, while asking us to remember the signs and follow them anyway. "There is enough light for those who desire only to see, and enough darkness for those of a contrary disposition." We are not Spock, dispassionately calculating the odds of attaining escape velocity from a black hole. We are more like Neo, deciding whether to trust Morpheus, or Ron Weasley, wondering whether to go on hunting Horcruxes with Harry and Hermione.

Pascal focuses on the moral component of faith not because we should will ourselves to believe "in the teeth of the evidence," but because fear or desire often cloud our minds. "Put the bottle down!" "Tar and nicotine blacken your lungs!" "He's the wrong guy for you!" In our addictions, we practice the absence of God. Returning to Him involves practical steps of faith, not to brainwash ourselves, but to clear our minds of the sins that cloud them.

Aslan warned of "thick air" as the children descended into Narnia. The Queen of Underworld made that air thicker by tossing incense on her fire, and strumming strings. Faith does not mean believing without evidence, but in the face of confusion, temptation, fear, and our personal or collective smoke screens.

Pascal urges the person in such a condition to "convince yourself, not by increase of proofs of God, but by the abatement of your passions." In other words, before you argue with the witch, first stomp on the fire. (Pascal will give "proofs of God" later in the book.)

Puddleglum's fire walk accomplished three things: the pain cleared his head, the witch began shrieking, and the travelers smelt burnt Marshwiggle, which was "not at all an enchanting scent." Pain, Lewis said in *The Problem of Pain*, is "God's megaphone to rouse a deaf world."

This is the necessary background to the "Wager." As Jill entered the lowlands, air thickened. Enchanted smog then pushed the Underworld Air Quality Index into "alert" territory. The witch's arguments were conducted under unfair sensual advantages, which had to be removed (like Sauron's ring) so counter-arguments could register.

Puddleglum's response was thus first practical, then logical. He sought to "abase passions" by a practical act. His mind having cleared, he conceded the strength of the witch's argument: true, my dislike for your pit of a kingdom may deceive me. But then he argued: "In that case, the made-up things seem a good deal more important than the real ones. Four babies playing a game can make a play-world which licks your real world hollow."

Here we find a petri dish within a petri dish. A hypothetical creature in an imaginary world invents a fictional reality to explain what we call the real one. Puddleglum actually offers two arguments, one implicit, the other explicit. Within the petri dish, we know that Narnia exists. The implicit evidence for it is the testimony of four people who claimed to walk, fish, dine, ride owls, shoot ducks, and run for their lives to avoid being made part of the gentle giants' Autumn Feast. The witch denies all this, but her testimony hardly counts, given her shaky track record. Anyway, we can only testify to places we have been, not to places we admit not having visited.

Explicitly, the marshwiggle says, it is a "funny thing" that four "babies" could invent a world more interesting than what an allegedly superior intellect could manage. (Here Lewis says he drew on the Ontological Argument of Anselm and Descartes, which, by the way, Plantinga later updated.) "Funny thing" here means not a "joke" or even a "proof," but "an interesting clue." It is the odd print that Columbo finds on the window pane, the bone Indiana Jones digs up, or the rock a geologist spots on the ice of Antarctica, that says, "someone has been here," or even "this comes from another world."

Puddleglum appeals to the third level of evidence: human (or marshwiggle) testimony. He also draws on more fundamental "ways of knowing:" memory, logic (the mind), and vision, hearing, taste, touch, and scent (the senses).

In effect, one can say that Puddleglum invites us to seek Christ through reason, but to be wary of the atmosphere of our times and passions. Make critical use of mind, senses, and human testimony. Like Pascal, he encourages us to remain aware of the value of the country we seek, the Pearl of Great Price.

Rilian rightly called Puddleglum an "honest wiggle." Like Pascal, he is at heart a scientist, investing in the research project called "life."

The Christian faith has always called us, as Jesus put it, to "Love the Lord your God with all your mind." Reason must rely on faith in mind, senses, people, and God, but faith must also be tested by reason. Pope John Paul II (another "p" to add to that pod of sound thinkers) compared faith and reason to two wings on a bird, both of which are needed for flight.

Science is now the most popular method for learning the origin of our world and why it contains life. Many students of history say faith in a rational Creator nurtured modern science into being. We can learn much about the origins of our world, and the creatures in it, from a song that a lion sang in a children's fantasy.

Suggested Reading

Beginning: For the next chapter, you should read *The Magician's Nephew*. Also recommended: *True Reason: Confronting the Irrationalism of the New Atheism.*

Advanced: C. S. Lewis: *Miracles, Pilgrim's Regress,* "Bulverism," "Transposition." I describe the four steps of faith in more detail in *Jesus and the Religions of Man.* You have to dig through some coal to find the many gems in Pascal's *Pensees,* but those gems are precious indeed. Two books by Alvin Plantinga shed light on faith and reason: *Where the Conflict Really Lies* and *The Ontological Argument from St. Anselm to Contemporary Philosophers.* My interview of Plantinga in *Faith Seeking Understanding: Essays in Memory of Paul Brand and Ralph Winter,* also touches on faith and reason.

TWO

The Lion's Song

"In the darkness something was happening at last. A voice had begun to sing. It was very far away and Digory found it hard to decide from what direction it was coming…Its lower notes were deep enough to be the voice of the earth herself. There were no words. There was hardly even a tune. But it was, beyond compare, the most beautiful noise he had ever heard…

"'Gawd!' said the Cabby. 'Ain't it lovely?'" *The Magician's Nephew*

I rest against the stump of a big-leafed maple. I just fought my way down a trail choked with blackberry vines to a bluff above where two forks of the Snoqualmie River converge. Melt from a late-winter snowstorm gurgles below. Fog partly shrouds the granite ramparts of Mount Si rising above the main fork. A young woman is walking along the far bank with a golden retriever, which plunges enthusiastically into icy ponds, and jumps up on fallen logs.

Perhaps a river god will poke his head up. Maybe Aslan will turn the retriever into the first talking dog. Even in the New Narnia, Lewis said that dogs "behave as if they thought whatever they were doing at the moment immensely important."

Such sentimental fantasies! You tell me. Look at the scene through scientific lenses! Will invasive blackberries choke out native species? What traits did dogs retain or lose as they descended from wolves, and wolves from previous carnivores? Is the Juan de Fuca plate, which thrusts under the continent to form these mountains, breaking into pieces? In what primordial stars, six times hotter than our sun, were helium atoms soldered into the carbon that forms the cellulose that holds those cottonwoods together, and then the larger oxygen that, mated with hydrogen forged in the Big Bang, flows below me now as habitat for rainbow trout?

Another day, I explore the Big Island of Hawaii. In the morning, I hitchhike to Kealakekua Bay, where Captain Cook was killed, and swim among turtles and brightly-colored, oddly-shaped fish. Then I rent a car and drive to Volcano National Park. Hundreds of people sit on a cliff above a black-sand beach, watching lava drop through steam into the sea. "God is still creating," someone says as we observe Kilauea's gentle eruption. After dark, I drive back over a road so high above sea level, and free of lights, that the stars shine more brightly than I have seen them before.

Is God still creating? Is He, or blind chance, responsible for all we smell and touch? Watch those stars! Listen to the waves breaking on black sands! Observe the basalt cool, steam rising as lava falls into the Pacific Ocean!

In *The Magician's Nephew*, Aslan sings a world into being. By listening to that song, I believe we can know better how waters, mists, beaches, thickets, canines, and humans came to be.

In the Beginning, Aslan

Digory, a boy in late nineteenth century London with, it seems, an inherited streak of scientific curiosity, discovers that his Uncle Andrew is a wizard. Andrew is unlike Dumbledore, though, or even Voldemort. He "works by rules and books," three fifths mud-blood at heart, one fifth scientist, the rest devil. He is a little Doctor Mengele, experimenting on animals, but happy to use humans when available. Andrew tricks Digory's friend Polly into taking a magical ring and vanishing "right out of this world." Digory loyally follows her, and the two children find themselves in a quiet park full of trees and ponds. At the bottom of each pond, they discover, lies a world. The children travel to a planet called Charn, and bring back Jadis, fully queen and four-fifths devil, who had exterminated every living creature on Charn but herself by means of the ultimate "weapon of mass destruction," a word of power, combined with proper formulae.

Through a series of misadventures, Digory, Polly, the uncle, the witch, a cab driver, and his horse all wind up in a third world, which at first is dark and silent, like a stage before the curtain rises.

"This is not Charn," says Jadis. "This is nothing."

Some scientists say our cosmos came from one or another kind of nothing. Physicist Lawrence Krauss wrote a book entitled, *A Universe from Nothing*. But the "nothing" before Narnia's creation cannot be absolute. After all, the party is standing on ground, which implies mass under their feet. And it takes oxygen to talk or croon (the cab driver tries to keep spirits up by singing a harvest hymn). Similarly, Columbia physicist David Albert pointed out that even if Krauss' theory were true, the universe must have begun with quantum fields out of which space and matter emerged. Philosopher of Science Stephen Meyer argues that quantum fields would require such careful engineering to produce universes that contain life, that it is simpler to suppose our universe just popped into being, because Krauss' theory would require it to defy odds so great they make "astronomical" a gross understatement.

A wilder song breaks the stillness. The music seems to come from the ground or sky. Stars suddenly brighten the firmament above, and "cold, tingling, silvery" voices sing harmony for a while. At the "mightiest and most glorious sound" of all, the sun rises.

A lion is seen pacing vaguely in the onlookers' direction. The music seems to be coming from him. He sings a "softer and more lilting" tune, and grass pours in waves across the landscape. Then plants follow: heather, beech, willow, lilac, wild rose, rhododendron, fir (following "deep, prolonged notes"). Primroses pop up to more lilting chords.

The music grows wilder still. The ground boils, and moles, dogs, deer, beavers, frogs, panthers, birds, butterflies, bees, and elephants emerge from seething mounds.

Finally the lion speaks:

"Narnia. Narnia. Narnia. Awake. Love. Think. Speak. Be walking trees. Be talking beasts. Be divine waters."

In the light of modern science, Christians disagree about Creation. Some say God made the world in six twenty-four hour periods a relatively short while ago. Others recognize (as Lewis did) that the world is old, but see a divine stamp on matter and life, a "signature in the cell," as Meyer put it. Others think God created so subtly that Nature carries no undeniable evidence of His activity.

But one fact is clear: our world, too, began in song. "In the beginning, was the Word," said St. John. That Word carried both harmony and rhythm. Scientists have decoded fragments of the music in the sixty-six years since *The Magician's Nephew* was published.

Aslan and the Big Bang

Stephen Hawking called it "The discovery of the century, if not of all time." In 1992, cosmic background radiation was detected in all directions, echoes of the explosion with which the universe began. Some scientists quailed at the idea that the cosmos had had a beginning. Geoffrey Burbridge complained of star scientists rushing off to join the "First Church of the Big Bang." Robert Jastrow, founder of NASA's Goddard Institute for Space Studies, said he was "fascinated" both by the discovery itself, and "because of the peculiar reactions of my colleagues."

Scientists found such harmonies built into space and matter that even the Uncle Andrews in the Physics Department found it hard not to tap their toes. The four fundamental forces of Nature seem exquisitely tuned to allow stars, planets, and molecules to appear. Carbon is formed in hot stars in a harmonic series called the "triple alpha process," that depends on fortunate resonances that allow three helium atoms to join quickly into one carbon. Without that bit of luck, we would live—or rather, not live—in a universe with only hydrogen and helium.

Water, whether in the Snoqualmie River or surrounding the Big Island, is one of the brilliant inventions of our universe. A water molecule contains one oxygen and two hydrogen atoms. Each oxygen pulls on the hydrogen in neighboring molecules, and its own hydrogen likewise flirts with adjacent oxygen atoms. This allows water to pack tightly, so it can liquefy at moderate temperatures, despite an atomic weight of just eighteen. So when water freezes, it doesn't contract like most compounds, but expands, creating the doom of the Titanic, but life for earthlings: ice that floats, rather than sinking and clogging rivers and seas.

"Simple" life is no mere blob of protoplasm, as once thought. A year before *The Magician's Nephew* was published, Francis Crick and James Watson interrupted lunch-time patrons at The Eagle pub in Cambridge to announce that they had discovered "the secret of life," the role DNA plays in coding for living creatures. Biologists continue to study the many giant leaps life had to take to set its footprints on Earth, let alone the Moon: learn to move, reproduce, form cellular power packs, photosynthesize, develop senses, bleed and know when and how to stop bleeding, and fill the microscopic tool shed of life with the thousands of complex proteins, cells, and organs required for all the tricks it has developed.

"Awake! Love! Think! Speak!" Michael Behe points out that in his *Ancestor's Tale*, Dawkins reverses the order of creation in Genesis (and the history of life), so that readers will not suppose that human beings are the goal of evolution. After all, a swift might see itself as the pinnacle of creation, because it flies further than any other bird. An elephant might perceive its magisterial nose as the biosphere's ultimate bragging point. Pascal knew better. "Even if the universe were to crush him, man would still be nobler than his slayer because he knows that he is dying..." Reason, not vanity, makes man the apex of earthly creation. It is I, not one of the gloriously antlered elk that graze in meadows nearby, who sits at this fork, and ponders Creation. Squid do not congregate at the beach in Hawaii and debate whether God is still making things.

Many who study the natural world hear a song. They speak of "the music of the spheres" (Johannes Kepler), a "cosmic symphony" (string theorist Brian Greene), or "the music of life" (Oxford systems biologist Denis Noble).

Noble, who studied the beating of the heart, compared life to polyphony, a music that weaves rhythms and melodies together. To write one good tune is tough. To join them together in harmony, as Bach did so masterfully, is far more challenging. In unguarded moments, whatever Force joined cells into organs, organs into bodies, and bodies into ecosystems, calls forth spontaneous praise even from hardened materialistic breasts. Harvard evolutionary biologist E. O. Wilson recalled standing on a ridge in New Guinea, watching birds circle in the setting sun:

> All that domain was bathed in an aquamarine haze, whose filtered light turned the valley into what seemed a vast ocean pool. At the river's edge 300 meters below, a flock of sulfur-crested

cockatoos circled in lazy flight over the trees like brilliant white fish following bottom currents. Their cries and the faint roar of the distant river were the only sounds I could hear. My tenuous thoughts on evolution, about which I had felt such enthusiasm, were diminished in the presence of sublimity. I could remember the command on the 4th day of Creation: 'Let the waters teem with countless creatures, and let birds fly above the earth across the vault of heaven.'

As the cab driver in newly-created Narnia put it: "I'd have been a better man all my days if I'd known there were things like this."

Consider a biologist with the attitude of Uncle Andrew surrounded, as Darwin put it, echoing the closing sentences of *Origin of Species*, by "endless forms, most beautiful and most wonderful." Even if one can trace a plausible evolutionary path from nothing to a planet full of those endless striking forms, would that really disprove the rationality of the song that brought life on this planet into being?

A few heretical scientists, like Behe, argue for a theory called Intelligent Design. In three increasingly skeptical books, Behe argues that many organs or cellular parts are "irreducibly complex," that they lie beyond the capacity of step-by-step Darwinian evolution to design. He believes that evolution does work, allowing an original pair of finches to diversify into a dozen or so species in the Galapagos Islands, and the perch-like fish called cichlids to grow into hundreds of species in the African Great Lakes over a few million years. But most of that evolution, he argues, comes by breaking genes, not by constructing new ones. He thinks natural processes by themselves can diversify species and genres, like dogs descending from wolves, but probably not create original classes or families.

In *Life Ascending*, evolutionary biochemist Nick Lane attempts to show how evolution allows living organisms to jump even the highest hurdles: the origin of life, sex, photosynthesis, and consciousness, among others. Not only unbelieving scientists like Wilson and Dawkins, but even many scientists who recognize a divine song in Creation, agree with Lane.

Lewis would have been fascinated by the debate. He usually deferred to practicing scientists and granted evolution "for the sake of the argument." But he insisted that whether or not science provided valid arguments for creation (he thought it might), Nature gave us a language of wonder by which to read the character of God.

I once asked Alvin Plantinga what questions in philosophy still piqued his curiosity. He said he thought there was good evidence for common ancestry (Behe agrees), but was curious how that fit in with the Christian idea of the Fall. "How much does the Lord intend us to take literally? And once you've got that figured out, how does that fit in, if at all, with current evolutionary theory?"

Some believing scientists say evolution should shock us more than a static view of Creation. William Paley famously compared organisms to a watch you find lying on the ground: it practically shouts (or ticks) "Someone made me!" Oxford physicist Ard Louis told me he sees evolution as like coming into a room and finding legos not already formed into airplanes or ships, but snapping themselves together. Dawkins called this process "The Blind Watchmaker." In *Modern Physics and Ancient Faith*, Stephen Barr noted with astonishment: "Paley finds a 'watch,' and asks how such a thing could have come to be there by chance. Dawkins finds an immense automated factory that blindly constructs watches, and feels that he has completely answered Paley's point."

I noted to Plantinga that even Dawkins sometimes seems "almost ready to drop to his knees in wonder before Creation." Plantinga agreed, observing, "But he doesn't want to drop to his knees.

For one reason or another, he's extremely opposed to doing that sort of thing, and he thinks no one should do it."

What the Narnian creation story gives us is not a new scientific theory, but a sense of wonder to see nothing turn into so much that is so amazing. That reflects a part of Lewis' life-long response to the natural world.

The Narnian Naturalist

Phillip Pullman praises what he calls The Republic of Heaven, a place where there is "no room for a Divine Creator." He likes the Gnostics because they portray God as a villain, as Pullman also does in *His Dark Materials*. But he accused Lewis of being a "paranoid bigot" and making Narnia a guide to what was "wrong and cruel and selfish" because his heroes escape to a "truer Narnia," rather than growing up and enjoying this world. But the reason the ancient Gnostics disliked God, was because He created the material world. Both Gnostics and Lewis borrowed from Plato's vision of this world as a cave that contains mere images of ultimate reality, not "the real thing." Pullman doesn't like that. He thinks that Tolkien's Middle Earth, too, is harmful because it has no connection to this world.

Pullman appears to be one of those people Lewis was describing when he wrote: "So many people cannot be brought to realize that when B is better than C, A may be even better than B. They like thinking in terms of good and bad, not of good, better, and best, or bad, worse and worst."

Stand, again, at the confluence of two forks of the Snoqualmie River. You may rejoice in every ripple of current, the mists, mountains, and trees, then say, "The God who created this world also created an ultimate home of which such visions are an image." That is not only different, it is the opposite from saying, as the

Gnostics would, "These fogs and vapors are a delusion created by the evil Yaltabaoth and subordinate archons!" Both may reference Plato, but the first leads on to Aristotle, Einstein, and Ansel Adams, the second to the paranoid isolation of The Matrix.

C. S. Lewis was fascinated by the natural world. He loved to walk with friends through the countryside in Oxfordshire, Cornwall, and Northern Ireland. He wrote to children about watching Venus and Jupiter cross the night sky; flooded meadows where his college's deer looked "miserable" until someone rescued them; a rabbit who yawned or took food from his hand; a hedgehog that snuck into his house, drank a saucer of milk, then "got into the saucer and settled down to sleep;" or a neighbor with a beard like a goat who stole his firewood, and whom, if he knew magic, he might turn into a goat. "It wouldn't be so very wicked because he is so like a goat already!"

As a child, Lewis was deeply moved by Beatrix Potter, creator of *Peter Rabbit* and a capable naturalist. He also enjoyed Lewis Carroll, who taught math at Christ Church, and took a girl named Alice to the Pitts River Museum, where a dodo bird was preserved.

Delightful as the country into which Alice's namesake fell was, it lacked two qualities to be a genuine "wonderland." First, it wanted laws. You never knew if you were about to grow or shrink, be attacked by playing cards, meet an arrogant egg or a caterpillar with a drug addiction. Without rules, one meets curiosities, but not true wonders. Dawkins and Behe disagree about evolution, but both find biological patterns all the more marvelous for following rules.

Like our world, Narnia is lawful. The land may not carry so much complex back-story as Middle Earth (an unfair standard!), but it is rational enough to awaken wonder. That, Chesterton wrote, is one purpose of fairy-land. Rivers in fairy tales run with wine, so we can be rightly astonished to see they run with water. Science helps reawaken that wonder.

Law, in Nature, means mathematical regularity. Science quantifies the music of creation. Scientists transcribe the orbits of planets and refraction of light in numbers. The ratio of dominant and recessive traits in peas, combinations of quarks that make atoms, and the orbits of moons, planets, and stars, are all harmonic—therefore numerical—tunes played in the medium of matter.

Second, Alice took her odd experiences in stride, as in a dream. That was right for Carroll's kind of story: as Lewis himself pointed out, the fun would have turned into a nightmare, if Alice got flustered every time she fell down a rabbit's hole or was sentenced to death by the Queen of Hearts. By contrast, the best scene in the first Narnia film is Lucy walking through the wardrobe door with delight and amazement on her face as snow swirls down in a forest empty but for the light of a lonely lantern. So my son, at one, crawled in fascination towards light on our apartment floor, at two pointed at cows and said "enu!" (the Japanese word for "dog"), and at four broke into gales of laughter to see a bushy-tailed squirrel run up a tree. Such "aha" experiences, like E.O. Wilson on that ridge in New Guinea, echo the moment of Creation.

The Ultimate Scientist

Aslan is the ultimate scientist because he does not just explain how a world emerges, but creates one. Historians likes Allan Chapman, James Hannam, and David Landes, show how natural philosophers came to believe in a Singer before they worked out the notes of His song. Some scientists in pagan Greece had also become believers in God, as the radical historian of ancient science, Richard Carrier, admits in *The Christian Delusion*: "Most intellectual polytheists believed in a Creator who had intelligently ordered the cosmos, that this order could be discovered by the human mind, and that such discovery honored God."

Some welcome the news of creation, because they believe in the Creator. Others hear the song, but like Uncle Andrew, hate and fear the Singer. Sure, the constants of Nature that allow life seem more carefully orchestrated than a concert with many instruments. (Some physicists give such odds against our universe's run of luck that it would take far more than a digit on every atom in the cosmos just to write that number out!) But the Singer is still deniable. Perhaps our Wood contains an infinite number of worlds, and we live in one in which natural melodies happened to form mountains, rivers, trees, and the talking animal called "man." Trillions of worlds are filled with white noise: we got lucky, the monkey at the piano played Handel for us. (Though Meyer argues forcefully against such theories.) We can sing our own Hallelujah Chorus; who needs a lion to solo?

Yet even many unbelievers hear the music, and love it. They watch animals emerge from the ground and clap hands in delight. They burrow into the hill to see where jackdaws came from.

Creation invites worship, but does not compel it. And for believers in a good God, it also raises difficult questions.

The Problem of Pain

Design theory seems to grow stronger, the more we learn. But whether Nature proves calculated or not, Lewis recognized that it speaks with an ambiguous voice. No canonical writer, Lewis noted (quoting Pascal) tries to prove God directly from Nature. Behe writes about the evolution of HIV, malaria, and the bacteria flagellum, which he insists not only looks like but actually is an outboard motor. Granted the appearance of design, why would God craft such nasty pests, though?

With the doctrine of Creation comes what Lewis called "the Problem of Pain." If God is good, why did he create a Nature in which dog eats dog, and we all battle the enemy Gollum described in a riddle he told in hopes of dining on one Bilbo Baggins?

This thing all things devours;
Birds, beasts, trees, flowers;
Gnaws iron, bites steel;
Grinds hard stones to meal;
Slays kings, ruins town,
And beats high mountains down.

"Time!" Bilbo squeaked, meaning "Give me more time!" But he was saved by luck, because time is the monster Gollum spoke of. Which means our luck in the cave of this world cannot last forever.

"No one died before Eve ate the fruit," you may reply. But Meyer wrote another long book describing the fossils of creatures that died 540 million years ago in the Cambrian Era. Adam did not kill them. Ralph Winter, the founder of the US Center for World Missions, was so troubled by pre-human suffering that he founded another institute, named after his wife who had died of cancer, to try to solve the problem. (He gamely bought me a plane ticket from London to a conference in Chicago to throw cold water on the solutions he and other participants proposed!)

Narnia does not answer this difficulty. Aslan does not sing ticks or viruses into being. Panthers emerge without pouncing on rabbits. Digory woke Queen Jadis. But Lewis doesn't tell us how ogres or hags arrived in Narnia, or the polytheistic, war-mongering Calormene Empire. Aslan does not clearly answer the question that troubles believers: in a universe of such beauty and wonder, whence come pain and death?

Lewis gives a few more clues in his adult tale about Mars, *Out of the Silent Planet*. The *hrossa* are seal-like singers and poets who live along the planet's canals, happy as Adam and Eve before the fall. But in those waters live shark-like creatures, *hnakrapunt*, that attack and sometimes eat hrossa. The hrossa do not see this aquatic monster as evil, but write poems celebrating its life story. Their own lives seem sweeter for the danger. They long to be in the forefront of hunting the creature, and sing songs about those lost to its jaws of death. In *Reflections on the Psalms*, Lewis notes that unlike the Norse or Greeks, the Jews also could take a "clear objective view—noting the lions and whales side by side with men and men's cattle." This came, Lewis argued, through the idea of God as "creator and sustainer of all," adding that Akhenaten, the Egyptian king who came close to inventing theism, showed some of the same attitude in his *Hymn to the Sun*.

The North Cascades between Mount Baker and Mount Shuksan is a gorgeous region of soaring mountains, turquoise lakes, and alpine gardens in which marmots dine on lupine and whistle among heather-covered boulders. But it was while being lost in those mountains, and "shivering under a stunted tree in a cold mixture of snow and rain," that Plantinga says he felt the presence of God most palpably. Death often seems to serve that function for humans as well as hrossa. If we were immortal, we would probably be as insufferable as Zeus.

Perhaps Lewis would have seen Nature in darker hues if he had lived in the Amazon jungle, among piranhas, snakes, scorpions, and clouds of disease-ridden insects. But no story is possible without *hnakrapunt*, dragons, furies, balrogs, death-eaters, vampires, White Walkers, or Black Riders. Life, like a flower, is more beautiful for its fragility. In that sense, all adventure stories help answer the "problem of pain." Without the White Witch, there would be no tale to tell.

Queen Jadis and Uncle Andrew are scientists of a sort. So are some of the villains in Lewis' *Space Trilogy*, like Dr. Weston, who planned to harm the hrossa on a larger scale than canal sharks ever could. If Lewis loved Nature, why did he sometimes make those who study it out to be the bad guys?

The Corruption of Science

The Empress Jadis "looked as if she understood the music (of Aslan) better than any of them," and hated it. Uncle Andrew, who had done "cruel experiments" on animals, feared them.

Lewis warned of how the ego may cannibalize innocence. Uncle Andrew was once doubtless a curious boy like Digory. Then lust for power went to his head. He aimed to colonize Narnia with machines, as the Emerald Witch sought to invade it with gnomes, Weston tried to colonize Mars, and Colonel Quaritch subjugated Pandora. (And historically, European nations had colonized most of the world.) Lewis hated bullying. This is why, when Arthur C. Clarke, author of *2001: A Space Odyssey*, invited him to a talk in London on extraterrestrial exploration, Lewis replied, "I wish your lecture every success except a practical realization of space travel!"

Clarke also griped, in private letters to Lewis, about the depiction of scientists in *That Hideous Strength*. John Haldane, the pioneer in evolutionary theory whom Lewis quoted on evolution and reason, and a friend of Clarke's, summarized what he took as Lewis' point:

"Mr. Lewis' idea is clear enough. The application of science to human affairs can only lead to hell."

Lewis replied that while science need not lead to hell, it certainly can.

Both Haldane and Lewis fought in World War I, when tens of thousands choked on newly-invented chemicals or were mowed down by machine guns. Communists and Nazis then glorified science and used it to kill masses of people in new ways. In our world, Jadis' words invoking holocaust were written in mathematical formulae. Aslan warned Digory and Jill against the doom of which Hiroshima and Nagasaki seemed harbingers:

> *"They looked and saw a little hollow in the grass, with a grassy bottom, warm and dry.*
>
> *"'When you were last here, that hollow was a pond, and when you jumped into it you came to the world where a dying sun shone over the ruins of Charn. There is no pool now. That world is ended, as if it had never been . . . It is not certain that some wicked one of your race will not find out a secret as evil as the Deplorable Word and use it to destroy all living things. And soon, very soon, before you are an old man and an old woman, great nations in your world will be ruled by tyrants who care no more for joy and justice and mercy than the Empress Jadis.'"*

The apple tree Digory planted, Aslan warned, would only keep the witch away from Narnia for a few hundred years. A Culture of Life eventually begins to wither. Men once sought power through Magic; now we find it by technology.

But Clarke and Haldane should not have read one fictional physicist or corrupt research organization as an indictment of science as a whole. Lewis recognized the sciences as "good and innocent in themselves," as he explained in *That Hideous Strength*.

A boy named Lawrence Krieg, born to an American diplomat in Venezuela, wrote Lewis, apparently asking why the author didn't like panthers. Lewis replied that actually he thought them "one of the loveliest animals there are" and only remembered putting good panthers in his stories. Aside from correcting Lawrence's premise, Lewis also challenged the logic of his ten year old critic (a future computer scientist): "Even if I had that wouldn't have meant that I thought all Panthers were bad, any more than I think all men bad because of Uncle Andrew, or all boys bad because Eustace (sic) was once a traitor."

Haldane is not the only "great intellect" who misreads Lewis as that boy did. As we will see, other famous thinkers claim that Lewis hated women because of Susan. Such critics commit the same errors both of fact—overlooking good women and scientists in Lewis' fiction—and of reason—generalizing from few to all for no good reason.

Yet as we gain power over Nature by splitting atoms and allowing pathogens far worse than any coronavirus to gain new functions, only a fool would say, "What, me worry?"

Lewis also worried about the power scientists wield over animals.

Uncle Andrew proudly described his experiments on guinea pigs: some died and some "exploded like little bombs." "It was a jolly cruel thing to do," said Digory. "That's what the creatures were for. I'd bought them myself," replied his uncle.

A stray cat kept a lonely runaway named Shasta company in the desert. Jackals began to howl. The cat left Shasta. Then he heard a lion roaring, and the jackals scampered off. As the lion returned, the boy shook in fear, but the animal seemed to shrink and shrink until…"I do declare it's only the cat! I must have dreamed about its being as big as a horse."

Shasta then confessed to the cat that he had once thrown rocks at an old stray, and the cat scratched him. "Hey, stop that! It's not as if you could understand what I'm saying."

The National Institute for Coordinated Experiments held stables full of animals that were "tortured" (said Merlin) for science. Or as Studdock put it, "thousands of pounds worth of living animality which the Institute could afford to cut up like paper on the mere chance of some interesting discovery." One of the heroes of that story was Bultitude the Bear, who fulfilled a prophesy by ripping the demon-possessed head of a French murderer off the wall. (Lewis had befriended a real-world Bultitude at Whipsnade Zoo an hour east of Oxford.)

Queen Jadis would not just have tortured a cat, or smashed a few kennels, but torn all worlds to pieces to stop Aslan's song. Narnia was no wonderland to her. Childhood curiosity had long since collapsed in on her ego, like a star into a black hole.

But Lewis' warning about how even love for truth can be corrupted was not just for scientists. In *The Great Divorce*, a theologian took a bus-ride from hell to heaven. There an old friend offered him a place "where you can taste truth like honey and be embraced by it as by a bridegroom. Your thirst shall be quenched." But the theologian denied any "thirst for some ready-made truth," and walked away from heaven, humming an old hymn. A landscape artist similarly abandoned heaven, and his former love of beauty, out of concern over fame on Earth.

So Narnia reveals science as an invitation to delight and wonder that can take us out of ourselves, and point us to the Creator. But because science lends power, it can also become "bad magic" that warps the soul, tortures creation, and tyrannizes man and beast. Indeed, any love is liable to turn from delight in the Other, to food for the expanding ego. Like an apple, science is good, but can tempt us to fall. Yet study of Nature is often the wardrobe through which those who thirst for truth find their way into Aslan's Country.

John Haldane need not feel put upon. For Lewis, we are all Adam and Eve, facing a whole orchard of temptations. So Aslan warns us against taking candy from power-hungry witches.

Suggested Reading

Beginning: For the next chapter, you should read *The Lion, the Witch, and the Wardrobe*. I cited *Mere Christianity* in this chapter, a wonderful introduction to the Christian faith. My *The Truth About Jesus and the 'Lost Gospels'* defends the Christian faith against Gnosticism and neo-Gnosticism, and is also an easy read.

Advanced: Michael Shermer's *Why Darwin Matters* is a good, short argument for evolution, while Nick Lane's well-written *Life Ascending* seeks plausible scenarios for some of the more difficult phases of that ascent. Richard Dawkins' *The Greatest Show on Earth* is more bombastic, but also well-written and with beautiful illustrations.

On the other side, while a bit outdated now, Hugh Ross' *The Creator and the Cosmos* tells the story of the Big Bang and the reaction to it well. Martin Rees' *Just Six Numbers: The Deep Forces That Shape the Universe* describes a few of the "coincidences" that allow for life in this cosmos. *Modern Physics and Ancient Faith*, by physicist Stephen Barr, offers a broader picture of God and cosmology. Michael Denton, *The Miracle of the Cell*. Michael Behe has written three books breaking new ground in favor of Intelligent Design: *Darwin's Black Box*, *The Edge of Evolution*, and *Evolution Devolves*. Stephen Meyer's *Signature in the Cell* and *Darwin's Doubt* are also worth reading. His newest book, *The God Hypothesis* is another slow-paced but thorough build-up to a persuasive argument. (He writes like General Grant fought.) Meyer argues that God is the best explanation for (1) the origin of the universe or multiverse; (2) of fantastically-improbable fine-tuning; (3) and of the equally incredible origin of life. Shermer and Meyer engage in a civil and enlightening debate on-line. Also cited in this chapter, but not named, is E.O. Wilson's engaging *The Naturalist*, and David

Albert's review of Krauss' book in the New York Times, "On the Origin of Everything,"

On God and the history of science, see James Hannam, *The Genesis of Science*; Allan Chapman, *Slaying the Dragons: Destroying Myths in the History of Science and Faith;* and Rodney Stark, *For the Glory of God*, Chapter Two: "God's Handiwork: The Religious Origins of Science." Also mentioned are David Landes, *The Wealth and Poverty of Nations*, Robert Jastrow, *God and the Astronomers*, and Richard Carrier, "Christianity was not Responsible for Modern Science," in John Loftus, *The Christian Delusion*.

THREE

Turkish Delight

"You simpleton! Don't you know what that fruit it? I will tell you. It is the apple of youth, the apple of life. I know, for I have tasted it; and I feel already such changes in myself that I know I shall never grow old or die. Eat it, Boy, eat it; and you and I will both live forever and be king and queen of this whole world—or of your world, if we decide to go back there." Jadis to Digory, *The Magician's Nephew*

"The Queen let another drop from her bottle fall onto the snow, and instantly there appeared a round box; tied with Greek silk ribbon, which, when opened, turned out to contain several pounds of the best Turkish Delight. Each piece was sweet and light to the very center and Edmund had never tasted anything more delicious." Jadis to Edmund, *The Lion, the Witch, and the Wardrobe*

Plato saw imagination as a tool of moral reasoning. In his *Republic*, Socrates challenged unworthy portraits of the divine: Kronos swallowing his sons, Zeus killing his father, the gods squabbling over Troy. "This is the reason why I am a defendant in the case," Socrates explained, "Because I find it hard to accept things like that being said about the gods." He was willing to die, because he agreed with his critics that educators held the future of Athens in their hands: "It is right to care first that the young should be as good as possible, just as a good farmer will likely take care of the young plants first."

What can Aslan teach young people about the good life? Does he corrupt the youth, as was said of Socrates, and as Philip Pullman claims? Or do ideas represented by Aslan, and the Gospel of Jesus, help people become "as good as possible?"

The Subversive Morality of Narnia

They say we evolved by clubbing, biting, fondling, and passing on our "selfish genes." Nature knits a bond between puppies in the same basket, so they can hunt rabbits together when they grow up. So why should Lucy care about a faun, or Digory about a talking lion? Narnians may not even have DNA, for all we know, and share no common ancestor with humans.

"What is the greatest commandment?" someone asked Jesus. In response, he offered a formula for morality as pithy as $E = MC^2$. (And that has worn as well.) "Love the Lord your God with all your heart, soul, mind, and strength," he replied. "And love your neighbor as yourself." All that is holy, he said, depends on these two fundamental kindnesses.

The questioner was a lawyer, though, and knew that good law can be as hard to apply as to formulate. "Who is my neighbor?" was his follow-up.

We are defined by how we answer that question. Plato said, "Your city." Hitler said, "Your race." Marx said, "Your class." Confucius said, "Humans, especially family, but not horses." Buddha said, "Humans, horses, horse flies, tigers, and lions, without discrimination." Princeton philosopher Peter Singer says, "Creatures who have attained a certain level of intelligence, less so fetuses or the mentally retarded."

Jesus offered a "legal precedent" that rings as universally true as the formula it illustrates: the story of the Good Samaritan. A man who belongs to our socio-racial-religious in-group was mugged on a deserted road. Two of our respected leaders came by, but ignored the man lying in a pool of his own blood: perhaps they had engagements, feared bandits, or didn't want stains on their suits. Then a despised outsider stopped, broke out his First Aid kit, patched the man up, and took him to a hotel. "Take care of this fellow, and I'll return and foot the bill," he told the manager.

How might that story apply to sentient non-humans, say talking mice or dwarfs? Two science fiction writers, Kingsley Amis and Brian Aldiss, came to visit C. S. Lewis in his rooms in Magdalene College, Cambridge one day. During the conversation, Lewis praised the "serious theme" of a story called "Food to All Flesh," by Zenna Henderson, which retold the story of the Good Samaritan, featuring monsters from outer space.

An alien craft lands in a semi-desert in North America. Out crawls a Momma creature and famished cubs. They meet a kind-hearted padre, who looks for something to feed the whelps. Nothing stays down, until one of the babies begins to suck blood from the man's veins. The mother carefully examines the padre and sadly decides she cannot nourish her child at the cost of an innocent person, however strange to her or lacking in common genetic material. The creatures climb back in their spaceship and take off.

As a follower of Jesus, Lewis agreed with the padre that we have a duty to "hnau," rational beings, whom we meet in need. (Samaritans were alien enough to the Jews.) And even asteroids, deserts, and glaciers are part of God's creation. If we love God, we should treat inanimate objects with respect. To the extent animals resemble man— in sentience, suffering, and nascent rationality— Jesus' story seems to make room for them, too. True, the Good Samaritan set the man on his donkey, not his donkey on the man. The Bible recognizes a hierarchy of duties to (a) relatives; (b) *hnau* we meet that are in need; (c) one's nation; and (a few verses add) (d) animals.

Jesus did not just offer moral formulae, he told a story to show what he meant. A story is "an experiment done with ideas," as Lewis wrote in an essay about the fantasy works of his friend, Charles Williams. "It's not what you are underneath, Batman. It's what you do that defines you." Abstract principles become incarnate in action, revealing grace or ugliness.

The GOAT of Temptation Stories

When it comes to girl-meets-talking-snake or boy-meets-witch stories, C.S. Lewis may have been the GOAT, the Greatest Of All Time. He had fed on *Dante's Inferno* and *Paradise Lost* all his life, and inherited his father's gift for "wheezes," and satire from his mother.

Lewis first came to popular notice as author of a series of letters from a senior to a junior devil on how to entice a young man to sin. Whether describing a bus trip from hell to heaven (*The Great Divorce*), illustrating the failures of affection, friendship, romance, and charity (*The Four Loves*), rerunning the temptation of Eve on Venus (*Perelandra*), or tracing the path of a sociologist entering a demonic "inner circle" (*That Hideous Strength*), Lewis' imagined worlds continue to shine light on that crucial next step, and where our choices might take us.

Lewis' greatest adult fiction, *Till We Have Faces*, is also about forks in the road. The heroine, Orual, is seen by her contemporaries as a great queen of a small ancient kingdom. Guided by a Greek philosopher (who teaches her reasoning) and a faithful warrior (who draws on her nation's myths and imagination), Orual applies science and compassion to rule her nation well over many years. But at heart, she is at war with the gods, whom she has hated since childhood. Her Solomonic works are a game she plays to keep the ghost of her beloved younger sister, Psyche, whom she ruined out of jealousy, from haunting her. She wears a mask to hide physical ugliness, as Adam and Eve clothed themselves in fig leaves to hide moral disgrace. Her greatest genuine virtue is that she takes justice seriously. She wishes, like Prometheus, and Pullman, to accuse the gods. But how can we meet the gods face to face, until we have faces? Orual needs to take off her mask, and own the ugliness of her soul, to gain true spiritual beauty and face the divine. Honestly "facing" the true character of one's soul is one of the great themes of Lewis' work.

Testing Virtue

Build an aircraft, and you want to take it up. Create a new species of rational being, and you may wish to put her soul under g-forces in the wind tunnel of life. Even before he became a Christian, Jack Lewis loved the poetry of John Milton, which described the temptation of Adam and Eve: "He is as voluptuous as Keats, as romantic as Morris, as grand as Wagner, as weird as Poe, and a better lover of Nature even than the Brontes." Lewis set his second space story on Venus (*Perelandra*), where the demon-possessed Weston tempted a green-skinned Eve to sin.

In a flask, you hold conditions constant (PH level, heat, salinity). Most Narnian characters are likewise set in their ways: Jadis' minions are predictably evil, while Reepicheep, Hwin the mare, and Trufflehunter the Badger ("I'm a beast, and we keep on"), are reliably good. Into dishes filled with predictable agents, Lewis placed the elements to be tested. Would Digory ring the bell or eat the apple? Would Lucy follow Aslan if everyone else slept in? Would Jill obey the signs, even in a snowstorm, or confronted with a madman?

Voyage of The Dawn Treader features a baton race of temptations. The focus shifts from Eustace (who keeps a diary, in which
he engages in passive-aggressive whining and justifies stealing water), to Lucy, on Dark Island and in the magician's home (where
she is tempted to cast "a spell to make beautiful her that uttereth it
beyond the lots of mortals.") Caspian picks up the baton and runs
the final leg, when he is tempted to abandon his crew (and future
wife) and voyage to the edge of the world. Jesus likewise endured
a trinity of temptations: to satisfy physical needs, gain power, or
engage in self-destructive exhibitionism.

The Magician's Nephew tells how Narnia came into being. It also
describes how an evil witch entered that world, brought accidentally (but not guiltlessly) by Digory, who then traveled to a distant
garden to pluck an apple to protect Narnia from the witch he had
let in. The apples were enticing, and Jadis encouraged him to steal
one for himself.

Temptation is often represented by succulent fruit. A witch offers
Snow White an apple. The Monkey King steals peaches that lend
immortality. St. Augustine recalls with shame how he and teenage
friends swiped pears from a neighbor's tree just for the mischief of
the act. Milton's devil describes the fruit that enticed Eve:

> Here grows the Cure of all, this Fruit Divine,
> Fair to the Eye, inviting to the Taste,
> Of virtue to make wise ...

Eve thought the magic must have worked: after all, the snake
ate first, and now he could speak! Neither had he died, as God had
warned.

Jadis, too, sampled the wares first. She also knew that the fruit
had given her lasting life: "It is the apple of youth, the apple of
life. I know, for I have tasted it, and I feel already such changes in
myself that I know I shall never grow old or die."

Jadis then dragged Digory through what psychologist Abraham Maslow might call a "hierarchy of temptations." First, Digory was enticed sensually (as Eustace was on the Dawn Treader, and Jesus in the wilderness). Then Jadis suggested that the two rule as "king and queen" of Narnia or of Earth (as Satan promised "the kingdoms of the world").

Digory held out against both temptations, and Jadis tried a more purportedly "compassionate" line. (As in *Paradise Lost*, Satan tempts Adam explicitly with love for his wife, but implicitly with loneliness and self-pity.) You can almost hear her asking, like Weatherman Phil in *Groundhog Day*, "This is how normal people talk, right?" She had killed her own sister, but perhaps remembered parents who had once cared for her. "What about this mother of yours whom you pretend to love so? Your home will be happy again. You will be like other boys."

To "be like other boys" involves what French academician Rene Girard called "memetic desire." The grass looks greener on the other side of the fence. A dog drops its own bone when it thinks the other dog has found a juicier one. Temptation is often competitive, like the struggle for the Ring of Power.

Digory circled this bait and was about to bite, when Jadis foolishly let slip her itchy old, virtue-signaling Covid mask of compassion. Ditch Polly! No one need know! Take your ring and fly back to England! The devil, Lewis proposed, clever as he may be, can slip up. He does not much understand love, for one thing. "All our research has yet to produce a virtue," admitted Screwtape.

But Digory was not yet a psychopath, and this "temptation" alerted him to Jadis' real aims. Suspicions, forgotten in grief (and the scent of the apple) were aroused. He remembered how Aslan had wept in the face of suffering. Jadis, by contrast, had long since exposed herself as a truly "jaded" character: nuking her home planet, beating cops, throwing Digory's aunt across the room, trying to kill a benevolent lion. "What's your game?" he asked.

It is the temptation of Susan, though, that most troubles Lewis' critics. While Orual knows herself to be ugly and covers her face, Susan knows she is beautiful, and uses lipstick to dress up as a "cover girl." In truth, hers is an honest story, and offers a warning to our increasingly vain and lonely world.

Northern Lights #1

"I'd like the pasta, please."

A portly man with a fringe of disheveled hair and piercing eyes passed the tray to a silver-haired, bearded gentleman by the window. The latter had been staring out the window (they were flying over western Greenland, and serrated peaks jutted dramatically above the fog, with glimpses of glaciers below). He took the food, shifting several small paperbacks to the chair between them. He bowed his head, then unwrapped the aluminum.

"That isn't the Chronicles of Narnia *you're reading, is it?"*

"You have good eyes! Yes, brushing up..."

"Do you teach Lit?"

"Well... we touch on most everything, by the end of the semester. But we begin with stories."

"Quite right! But that Lewis stuff is airplane food for the mind! It is especially traumatic for young women. Poor Susan! Why don't you let your students chew on this, instead?"

"'The Subtle Knife?'"

"Second in the series, but the only copy I have on me."

"Thank you! I'll return it when we arrive at CHAZ International."

"Oh, keep it! I have other copies!"

The old man took a few bites of his salad, then turned and asked:

"What do you mean, 'poor Susan?'"

"Have you read The Last Battle? *Ghastly story. Lewis sends his heroine to hell for wanting to grow up and wear lipstick!"*

"You don't say! I don't remember that detail. I'll have to read it again!"

Is Susan a Lost Soul?

Philip Pullman's famous children's series begins with *Northern Lights* (or *Golden Compass*), and continues in *The Subtle Knife* and *The Amber Spyglass*. His is a Gnostic world. In it, "God" is a senile and weak creature, propped up by the Church. One might also call such a view "Promethean." The ancient Greek Aeschylus wrote a play called *Prometheus Bound*, about the titan Prometheus who gave gifts to mankind. He was punished by Zeus by being chained in the Caucasus Mountains, where an eagle came and pecked his liver every day. Karl Marx was deeply moved, as a young man, by Percy Shelley's poetic remake of that story, *Prometheus Unbound*, and quoted the ancient version in the prefix to his doctoral dissertation: "Better do I deem it to be bound to this rock than to spend my life as Father Zeus' faithful messenger,"

Pullman called the Narnia series "one of the most ugly and poisonous things I've ever read," accusing Lewis of a "life-hating philosophy." He would forever "detest the supernaturalism, the reactionary sneering, the misogyny, the racism, and the sheer dishonesty of (Lewis') narrative method." What Lewis calls "temptation," Pullman sees as natural feelings. Institutions create evil by suppressing positive emotions. "Every church is the same: control, destroy, obliterate every good feeling," as an enlightened witch puts it in *Amber Knife*.

The fate of Susan enraged Pullman:

> Susan, like Cinderella, is undergoing a transition from one phase of her life to another. Lewis didn't approve of that. He didn't like

women in general, or sexuality at all, at least at the stage in his life when he wrote the Narnia books. He was frightened and appalled at the notion of wanting to grow up."

For a man who refused to grow up, C. S. Lewis left quite a bio. He fought for his country, being injured by friendly fire. He became one of the most popular lecturers at Oxford, a conscientious tutor who deeply influenced brilliant students. He wrote works of profound and erudite scholarship. He enjoyed deep friendships, kept house, paid taxes, and aided the poor in secret. In an essay on writing for children, Lewis argued that "growing up" should not mean leaving typically "childish" pleasures behind:

> I now like hock, which I am sure I should not have liked as a child. But I still like lemon-squash. I call this growth or development because I have been enriched: where I formerly had only one pleasure, I now have two…I now enjoy Tolstoy and Jane Austen and Trollope as well as fairy tales and I call that growth…

I expect Lewis would have enjoyed Pullman's books, despite the man's preference for demons, witches, and shamans over God. In "Is Theology Poetry?," Lewis argued that bad beliefs often inspire good art. He saw Percy as a great poet and Aeschylus as a great dramatist. But anyone with a puppy and a nice carpet knows that urges do need to be controlled. As Chesterton put it in his critique of George Bernard Shaw, the philosophy of letting children learn by doing ends when your child approaches a cliff.

J. K. Rowling does not sic so many rhetorical dementors on Aslan, but is also troubled by the fate of Susan. Harry Potter has girlfriends, even engages in "snogging." Why shouldn't Susan slap on some lipstick and go meet better boys than Rabadash the Ridiculous?

Like Krieg's complaint that Lewis hated panthers, such objections are both wrong in fact and unsound in logic. Susan was pursued by many beaus in Narnia. No one questioned her right to flirt, only whether she flirted with the right fellow.

Pullman and Rowling should reread Snow White, which Pullman included in an anthology of Grimm fairy-tales he put together. Wilhelm Grimm's version of the story is a profound Christian allegory of temptation and salvation, a warning not just to Susan, but to all "half-hearted creatures" who, as Lewis put it, are "too easily pleased…fooling about with drink and sex and ambition when infinite joy is offered us." Snow White's story reminds us that healthy growth often means self-limitation.

Snow White is unselfconsciously beautiful, lacking the vanity of her step-mother. When the queen tries to kill her, the girl flees to the home of seven dwarves who own seven candlesticks. They represent the Church, duty-bound to shelter those in danger. (Though power corrupts every institution, as Lewis warned, and Jesus before him.) The queen masks her outer beauty with her truer inner ugliness, dressing up as a hag, and tempts the girl three times: with a comb, beautiful laces, and finally, a poisoned apple. The first two, like Susan's stockings and lipstick, are not temptations to love or even lust, but to vanity, a cheap pretense of maturity before its substance has been attained. Like Susan, Snow White gives in, falling down "as if dead." But the dwarves take the comb out and untie the laces, and the girl revives.

Then Snow White eats the poisoned apple, and falls down not "as if dead," but "dead, and she remained dead." She is watched over by an owl, a raven, and a dove, which represent the wisdom of Greek, German, and Jewish cultures. Finally a prince appears (you can guess who he represented for Wilhelm Grimm, a pious Lutheran), and revives her. She "grows up" by overcoming temptations, tutored by the Church, and watched over by the sympathetic muses of diverse traditions. How could Pullman tell the story of

Snow White's laces and comb, rave about the Grimms, yet complain about Susan's lipstick and nylons?

Pinning our Sins

In *The Great Divorce*, hell disgorges a busload of day-trippers onto the outskirts of heaven. The visitors are encouraged to stay if they like: but tempted in various ways, all but one choose to "reign in hell" (a rainy suburb) rather than "serve in heaven" (a beautiful parkland).

Lewis recommended William Law's *A Serious Call to a Devout and Holy Life* to a needy American correspondent named Mary Shelburne: "You'll find all of us pinned like butterflies on cards— the cards being little stories of typical characters in the most sober, astringent eighteenth century prose."

Aside from Lewis' livelier style, that is a good description of *The Great Divorce*. Humans are pinned like butterflies by our fears, lusts, obsessions, apostasies, even mother love (swollen into an "uncontrolled and fierce monomania"). A wife demands renewed control over the husband she has dominated all her life: "I must have someone to— do things to. How can I pay him out if you won't let me have him?" A dwarf holds a drama king on a chain, the "false self" or mask he uses to blackmail those around him with pity. Materialists seek to prove that heaven is a hallucination. A "hard-bitten" ghost was blasé when he toured Beijing, Egypt, and Niagara Falls on Earth, and now posts one-star reviews of both heaven and hell. Other ghosts wish, like Uncle Andrew, to "dam the river, cut down the trees, kill the animals, built a mountain railroad, smooth out the horrible grass and moss and heather with asphalt." Napoleon paces back and forth endlessly, repeating: "It was Soult's fault. It was Ney's fault. It was Josephine's fault. It was the fault of the Russians. It was the fault of the English."

Richard Lenski froze daily samples of twelve tribes of E. coli to record different stages of their evolution. In Narnia, Lewis likewise freezes characters into states of sin: witches, conceited tyrants, lazy bureaucrats, passive-aggressive apes drunk on oranges and nuts, uncles with rings that hum ominously. Like all good villains, they know how to trash-talk: *"Scum! You shall pay dearly for this when I have conquered your world!" "Dare to touch my fire again, mud-filth, and I'll turn the blood to fire inside your veins!" "The bolt of Tash falls from above!" "Baby! Silly bleater! Go home to your mother and drink milk!"*

Names in *That Hideous Strength* reveal similarly fossilized characters: Wither, Frost, Curry (who curries favor in school politics), Lord Feverstone (hard, hot, and greedy), Miss Hardcastle (a cigar-chomping dominatrix with a taste for torture). In Narnia, villainy often debuts on a small screen first: Andrew cheating his sister, Rabadash kicking the Grand Vizier's bottom under the couch, the ape manipulating Puzzle the donkey's good will in order to enslave him, deft but simple sketches with touches of low comedy.

The point is not to gloat in watching beetles writhe under their pins—or sins—but to help us unstick ourselves, so we can fly free. Setting us free is also the point of the Gospel, not to rob the job from life, as Philip Pullman supposes. Who is more likely to succeed in life? Children who read Lewis and Tolkien and become cheerful prudes, like Mr. and Mrs. Beaver? Or children who read *His Dark Materials*, explore the delights of sex in their early teens like Lyra and Will, and wind up looking after children while their friends are in grad school? Scholars speak of a "success sequence," which divides winners from losers and explains why Asians are the most successful community in American society. Unlike Lewis, by scoffing at self-control and traditional morality, Pullman teaches young readers to lose the game of life.

Northern Lights II

The 787 dipped its starboard wing to reveal Flathead Lake, the mountains of Glacier National Park, with a dusting of new snow on higher peaks, rising beyond. The bearded gentleman stared out the window, then opened his mouth and pounded the window sill. The portly passenger in the aisle seat glanced over.

"Fly often?"

"It has been a while. And our previous ... craft ... flew closer to the ground."

"Enjoy my book?"

"Are you the author? An exciting read, to be sure! Your Lyra comes wonderfully alive."

"Thank you!"

"You ding God in the head with quite a rock, though! Do you think He noticed?"

"Heh. All bossy authorities, really. I was no fan of Soviet hierarchy, either."

"Pardon me for asking. But do you think it wise to teach children to blame institutions for the world's evil? I mean, Oxford itself, where Lyra is given her truth-o-meter, was once a Church institution. The place has had its uses, has it not?"

"Once scholars began to liberate themselves from rote indoctrination! Are you familiar with the history of the Enlightenment?"

The window passenger laughed. "Enough to doubt common accounts of it. And as a teacher, I find that young people not only need to be chastised from time to time, they welcome it."

"That sounds a little masochistic! Look, a jet cabin is not a good place to debate children's education. But I'm participating in a seminar on Capitol Hill Friday night. If you're staying in Seattle, why don't you join us? ... I'm sure other participants would love to hear your perspective." The aisle passenger grinned.

"*That is where I am headed. As an agent... (the old gentleman smiled brightly) of the Magisterium.*"

"*What! You're not defending* Narnia, *are you?*"

"*Yes I am! And I have to say, as imaginative as your book is, I did not find it as true to life as* Snow White and the Seven Dwarves, *let alone* Narnia.*"

"*Hmmm! You like all that sappy supernaturalism?*"

"*My problem is more mundane. Not to be rude. But when it comes to history, you could do with one of Lyra's truth-o-meters.*"

The aisle passenger snatched his book back. "I'll see you on Friday night!"

Suggested Reading

Beginners: C. S. Lewis: *The Great Divorce, The Four Loves.* "Food to All Flesh" can be found in a book of short stories by Zenna Henderson, *The Anything Box.* Next chapter: Please read *The Horse and His Boy.*

Advanced: C. S. Lewis: *Till We Have Faces, The Great Divorce, Perelandra.* Dante, *The Inferno*; Milton, *Paradise Lost*; M. Scott Peck, *People of the Lie.* Pullman's views of Lewis and Tolkien can be found in various chapters of *Daemon Voices: On Stories and Storytelling,* also in on-line articles. The conversation between Amis, Aldiss, and Lewis can be found in *Of Other Worlds.* G. K. Chesterton, George Bernard Shaw and Ronald Murphy, *The Owl, the Raven and the Dove: The Religious Meaning of the Grimm's Magic Fairy Tales.*

FOUR

Interview with a Lion

"At the name of Aslan each one of the children felt something jump in its inside. Edmund felt a sensation of mysterious horror. Peter felt suddenly brave and adventurous. Susan felt as if some delicious smell or some delightful strain of music had just floated by her. And Lucy got the feeling you have when you wake up in the morning and realize that it is the beginning of the holidays or the beginning of summer." The Lion, the Witch, and the Wardrobe

Some meetings define one for life. You wait for that girl or boy at the corner coffee shop; will you be opening presents around a tree amidst a gaggle of bouncing grandchildren forty years hence? You slip into a circle of desks surrounded by managers and teachers. Will you be festooning a room down the hall with posters, a cutout of Princess Leia, and a picture of Albert Einstein sticking his tongue out? You are ushered into the interrogation room, and a tape set on the table. Will you ever breathe free air again?

"Do you not know" Pontius Pilate asked Jesus, "That I have authority to crucify or release you?" "You would have no such authority, unless it had been given you from above," Jesus replied.

It is a common mistake. We go in for an interview, but forget who is judging whom.

He was a Jewish follower of the Cynic school, some say. Rabbi with a flair for rhetoric. Revolutionary who spoke for the poor and downtrodden. An image of a dying and rising god borrowed from common Near Middle Eastern mythologies. "Hippy in an Augustan age of yuppies." Prophet who foretold the coming of Mohammed. Guru who learned levitation and healing from Hindu ascetics. Zen Buddhist strolling the mean streets of Palestine like a kung fu master from the Shaolin temple wandering the old West.

Aslan reminds us that when meeting him, the shoe is on the other foot. No matter if you are a witch, prince, lonely dragon, conceited war horse, skeptical dwarf, or a girl showing off on the edge of a cliff. Aslan's eyes are a mirror to your soul. They see you with the clarity of your creator, who in the case of Narnian characters, was C. S. Lewis.

Jesus also seemed to see those he met with the clarity of their Creator, who was God.

"Meetings with Aslan" often echo the gospels. Like Eustace, Zacchaeus was a dragon, cut off from his own people, before he met the Lion of Judah and was transformed. Like Shasta and Jill, the Woman at the Well came to Jesus thirsty.

People were redefined by those interviews. Jesus called an audacious but crestfallen fisherman "The Rock." Respected religious leaders became a "generation of vipers." A poor widow of no account was revealed as the Giving Pledge heroine of ancient Israel. A Samaritan outcast with a string of failed relationships became her town's Billy Graham, sharing "living water" with her neighbors. Nickel investors were given keys to cities. Fishermen were told to start catching men for the Kingdom of Heaven. Those typecast before Christ (BC) as "Pharisee," "leper," "tax collector," "whore," or "thief," emerged from interviews with Christ (AD) with new identities based not on socio-racial-economic categories, but on Who they now knew.

Digory asked Aslan for a fruit to make his mother well. But like Jesus, Aslan seldom answered a direct question directly. He turned to the crowd of talking animals and announced: "This is the boy who did it."

"The boy who did it." "The boy who lived." "The bat who rescued Gotham." Digory was defined by what he had done, and by a family origin story: "Son of Adam. There is an evil witch abroad in my new land of Narnia. Tell these good Beasts how she came here."

This "son of Adam" might become "the boy who protected Narnia." But Digory's first experience of Aslan was of One who saw him better than anyone.

Before Nathaniel joined his band, Jesus said, "I saw you under the fig tree." Likewise, Aslan had long had his eyes on the cabby who would serve as the first king of Narnia:

"Son. I have known you long. Do you know me?"

"Well, no sir. Leastways, not in an ordinary manner of speaking. Yet I feel somehow, if I may make so free, as 'ow we've met before."

That Aslan knew "King Frank" in his London career reveals both characters. Frank is not a ghost like the partially-damned souls in *The Great Divorce*, on whom light gains little purchase. Odd, Lewis noted, how an all-knowing God could tell people He created, "I never knew you." Evil puts on an invisibility cloak that even the eyes of God cannot penetrate: "the door is shut from the inside." Frank, by contrast, is becoming human: he is rough, uncouth, disappointed in life, yet nurtures a seed of truth within. Aslan gives that sprout space to grow. "You have been faithful in a little. Now your kingdom extends from the Lantern Waste to the Sea."

Who so elegantly recreates the lives of those he meets? Perhaps the One who created us in the first place.

But in Narnia, we learn that "re-creation" can be a slow process. "Every year you grow, you will find me bigger." While Aslan knows us at that first interview, it takes longer to get to know him. For "Doubting Thomas," knowledge of Jesus grew through a wrenching series of trials and uncertainties. "Unless I see the print of the nails in his hands, and touch the scars with my fingers," Thomas demanded, "I will not believe."

Trumpkin, the Doubting Thomas of Narnia.

Four children and an honest but wary dwarf are lost in the woods. In the middle of the night, the youngest child wakes the others up, says she's met the great lion, and insists that everyone follow him. They peer in the darkness and see nothing. Grudgingly, they climb from sleeping bags, hoist packs, and trudge uphill, then over a cliff. One by one, the others begin to make out the shape of a lion padding ahead in the moonlight. Susan and Trumpkin are grumpiest about the midnight scamper, and slowest to see what they wish to deny. Trumpkin had scoffed at talk of long-lived lions: both his feet were firmly planted in his own version of Underworld. Aslan tosses Prince Caspian's self-possessed political adviser into the air, like a cat playing with a mouse, and asks, "Shall we be friends?"

Trumpkin's skepticism about lions leads to rough treatment when he meets one. But that man-handling (or dwarf-handling) is best understood as what Lewis described (in a powerful letter to a young friend who idolized, then lost, his wife) as a "severe mercy."

Thomas wants to see and touch his old Master? "Let him hear My Voice, too." Trumpkin's doubts were likewise challenged tri-sensually: by sight, voice, and paws grasping skin. An early biography says Thomas died founding the Church of India. Trumpkin helped save Narnia. Aslan deepened their faith and prepared them for those coming trials by allowing them to experience him with multiple senses, searing the memory of those meetings in their minds.

Confucius said, "If one learns the Way in the morning, then dies in the evening, that is enough." It is enough, because a meeting with The Way (as Jesus called himself) can instantly transform a jumble of confusing past events into a coherent life story.

Shasta Debates a Voice

Shasta is a displaced person, a refugee from Calormen with no bank account or passport, and few friends. He wanders a mountain pass into Narnia feeling sorry for himself. After all, he grew up without knowing his family, living in the shack of a Calormene fisherman who treated him like a slave. He ran away with a talking horse, but repeatedly encountered vicious lions on his journey. Now, while his friends are resting in a quiet compound with a kindly hermit, he must run on alone to warn King Lune of a Calormene invasion. But the horse the king lent him lags behind. His new "friends" gallop to safety in Anvard, while he is left wandering across another national border alone, aside from that useless steed.

Or are they alone? Some massive creature seems to be padding along in the fog to their left, paralleling Shasta's path. Then he hears it breathe deeply.

"Who are you?" Shasta squeaks out.

"One who has waited long for you to speak!"

"You're not something dead, are you? Oh, please—please do go away. What harm have I ever done you? Oh, I am the unluckiest person in the whole world!"

At this point, Shasta's curiosity is practical, not scientific or religious. He is not asking, as the bulldog asked Uncle Andrew:

"Now, sir. Are you animal, vegetable, or mineral?" He means, "Will you eat me?" Shasta is tired, hungry, and discouraged, and does not need "rough treatment" like Rabadash, Trumpkin, or (sometimes) St. Peter. As often in the gospels, the Voice reveals itself through dialogue: "Tell me your sorrows."

Shasta offers a depressing version of his life-story, but the Voice doesn't buy it: "I do not call you unfortunate." Shasta then unconsciously makes the same move as the Woman at the Well in John 4: he shifts the spotlight from his own troubles, to the identity of his conversation partner. "But what about all those lions we met?"

The Voice takes that word "lion" and ties the threads of Shasta's life together, while giving his life meaning in light of a larger story:

> "I was the lion who forced you to join with Aravis. I was the cat who comforted you among the houses of the dead. I was the lion who drove the jackals from you while you slept. I was the lion who gave the horses new strength of fear for the last mile so that you should read King Lune in time. And I was the lion you do not remember who pushed the boat in which you lay, a child near death, so that it came to shore where a man sat, wakeful at midnight, to receive you."

After Jesus calmed the waters, the disciples forgot their fears and stuttered, "Who is this man?" Shasta asks the same question: "Who are you?"

"Myself," the lion answers three times, "deep and low so that the earth shook," "clear and gay," and then softly.

This answer echoes the famous "I am" sayings in the Gospel of John. "I am the Bread of Life." "I am the Light of the World." It is an invitation to empirical discovery. Jesus cannot be encapsulated by titles—"teacher," "prophet," "Messiah," "son of man," "son of God." Look. Taste and see. In the Old Testament, another self-pitying servant of God met an earthquake, a fire, and a "mighty wind" that shattered rocks. But while God caused those events, He was "not in" them. Rather, he spoke to a tired and discouraged Elijah in a "still, small voice." So, too, Aslan finally whispers to Shasta: "Myself."

The lion disappears, leaving a deep footprint in the ground. The print fills with water, which forms a stream and runs downhill. Shasta drinks, then splashes his head: "It was extremely cold, and clear as glass, and refreshed him very much."

Of course Lewis "saw to the heart of each character" because he made them up, and put that knowledge into the mind of Aslan, whom he also invented. Is that why Jesus could see into the hearts of those he met— because the gospels are also fiction? If Lewis could make up such stories, why couldn't the first Christians?

Aslan told Sons of Adam and Daughters of Eve that knowing him a little in Narnia, they could come to know him better in our world. Lewis often told young people who wrote him, "Children see who Aslan is, but adults don't." Lewis drops clues in Narnia to help even Trumpkins who study the New Testament skeptically for a living find the real Aslan, whom no one could invent. "Aslan" invites us to play the role of Trumpkin, to look hard, reach out our hands, and ask tough questions, too.

Liar, Lunatic, Lion— or Legend?

C. S. Lewis put his most famous, and debated, argument for Christianity in the mouth of a professor talking about an imaginary world. That argument has to do with how we evaluate people (or fauns or lions) whom we meet.

Like Lewis himself, Professor Kirke served the war effort by playing host in his country home to children sent away from towns vulnerable to the German Blitz. Four sometimes squabbling brothers and sisters showed up. One rainy day, the kids played Hide and Seek. The youngest girl, Lucy, claimed to have discovered a world inside a wardrobe. The youngest boy, Edmund, teased her relentlessly, but she refused to back down. She had had tea with a faun. It was snowing, and she heard of a witch who turns people to stone.

Was Lucy going mad? Or turning into a "most frightful liar?" The two older children went to their host for feedback, but he floored them with a bizarre suggestion: "How do you know your sister isn't telling the truth?"

Professor Kirke's logic was simple. What do they teach them in these schools? Given the character of her claims, either Lucy was lying, or she was mad. Or she was telling the truth, and Narnia was real. But she was not mad, and didn't tell lies. So down the rabbit hole we may leap. Or mind our own business.

Lewis famously offered the same options about Jesus, in an argument for Christ's divinity known as the "trilemma." (Which he first gave in broadcast talks on the BBC during World War II, and then became part of his most famous apologetic work, *Mere Christianity*.) Given the extraordinary claims Jesus made about himself, our choices are limited, Lewis argued: "A man who was merely a man and who said the sorts of things Jesus said wouldn't be a great moral teacher. He'd either be a lunatic—on a level with the man who says he's a poached egg—or else he'd be the Devil of Hell."

In *The God Delusion*, Richard Dawkins challenged the trilemma: "A common argument, attributed among others to C. S. Lewis (who should have known better), states that, since Jesus claimed to be the Son of God, he must have been either right or else insane or a liar: 'Mad, Bad, or God.' Or, with artless alliteration, 'Lunatic, Liar, or Lord.'" Dawkins replied that actually, Jesus might have been "honestly mistaken." Anyway, "The historical evidence that Jesus claimed any sort of divine status is minimal."

Dawkins seemed bewildered at the ease of his victory. Surely as an experienced literary critic, Lewis had considered that the authors of the gospels might be spinning a yarn? Did the great apologist really fall into so simple and obvious a trap? Was his most famous argument for the Christian faith just a false choice?

Or did Dawkins overlook the Elephant (or Lion) in the room?

Lewis at the BEEB

On February 1st, 1942, Lewis first offered his "trilemma" to the British people on air.

Lewis knew his message had to be simple to be understood by most listeners. He also had to be concise because the program was limited for time. In *C. S. Lewis at the BBC*, Justin Phillips explained that Lewis originally meant to address the possibility that the gospels are unreliable accounts of what Jesus said about himself, and offer this rebuttal: "The theory only saddles you with twelve inexplicable lunatics instead of one."

Even if Lewis had had time to briefly mention and rebut that fourth "L," legend, it probably wouldn't have helped. True, Lewis was appealing to what scholars call a "criterion of historicity." If one child says she visited Narnia, you'd be gullible to believe. But if four children tell you stories that match, they are either colluding, or share a true common experience.

But we don't have reports from a dozen or even four disciples. We have four gospels, which many scholars say were written anonymously. Why should we believe what they quote Jesus as saying? Isn't it simpler to suppose that stories about Jesus passed from person to person and evolved along the way? Maybe the whole tale came from one person, as did the *Chronicles of Narnia*. Mark wrote the first version of the story down, then Luke and Matthew borrowed and amplified his errors. The famous New Testament scholar Bart Ehrman compares this process to a game of Telephone or Chinese Whispers, in which a group passes an original sentence around in a circle, also across cultural boundaries, and it comes out amusingly altered by the end. So John turned Jesus into a demigod, and western civilization was fooled.

True, John is most famous for a "high christology," showing us a Jesus who clearly speaks as if divine. However, the Gospel of John is not alone in presenting Jesus as more than human. Carefully read the "Sermon on the Mount" in Matthew, which deeply influenced Tolstoy and Gandhi. It is not just that Jesus casually upended the cruel morality of the Romans. Nor even that he one-upped the Stoics, who (even more than the Buddhism of the *Dharmapadda*) created the most soaring Gentile ethics. "You have heard it said…But I say…" Jesus also casually assumed authority to rewrite his nation's sacred scriptures. Confucius never dared to be so audacious. Even more astonishing, Jesus' version really is a radical improvement! "Therefore, anyone who hears these words and acts on them, may be compared to a wise man, who built his house upon the rock." The authority of Jesus is not tacked onto the gospels: it is woven through their fabric, in casual utterances, asides, and background assumptions, bonded as firmly as iron in stainless steel. And a "high Christology" is also implicit in how lives are recreated by a meeting with Jesus, throughout the gospels.

Lewis made the "trilemma" argument not despite, but because of, his rich knowledge of literature and astute judgment. Critics overlook an essay in which he not only showed why the "legend" hypothesis is unbelievable, but refuted much New Testament criticism decades before it was written. Like Trumpkin rubbing his eyes, or Andrew stopping his ears, many scholars blind and deafen themselves to the qualities in the gospels that prove Jesus' historical reality.

The Elephant and the Lion

C. S. Lewis held two great advantages over the writers of the gospels. First, he was a literary genius who knew the best that human invention had produced. When he was about sixteen, his astute tutor, William Kirkpatrick, already noted in a letter to Lewis' father: "Clive is an altogether exceptional boy. The maturity of his literary judgements is remarkable, he follows his own instinct and is not to be imposed upon by the mere weight of authority ... "

As an adult, whether tackling Spenser, Milton, or Hamlet, explaining Medieval love literature, offering a theory of how people read, or writing his great history of sixteenth century literature, when it looked like Lewis stood against the world, the world learned to listen. Lewis had a long track record of noting important facts about literary works that others failed to see. The famous critic and playboy Kenneth Tynan said he considered Lewis "the greatest English literary critic of this century and one of the best writers of English prose who ever lived."

Second, Lewis noted how easy it had been to write letters from the devil (*The Screwtape Letters*), and how hard it would be to write a corresponding set of letters from a heavenly vantage. To sound like hell, just suppress your conscience. Angelic correspondence would need to breath the very air of Heaven. Because they were written first, a later genius could borrow from the gospels to describe a figure who resembled Jesus in some ways. But Lewis knew that creating the portrait of Jesus in the gospels lay far beyond his own extraordinary abilities.

Fernseed and Elephants

In an address to an Anglican training school at Cambridge in 1959, Lewis began a critique of liberal Jesus scholarship by admitting that he was not well-read in the field. However, he cited five New Testament scholars (Rudolf Bultmann, Alfred Loisy, Ernest Renan, Paul Tillich, and Alec Vidler) and explained why, as a classicist who helped midwife some famous modern literature, his skepticism was "father to the ignorance": "It is hard to persevere in a close study when you can work up no *prima facia* confidence in your teachers."

Lewis was especially critical of Rudolf Bultmann, whose works A. N. Wilson drew upon in his biography of Jesus.

Lewis offered four criticisms. First, he claimed that liberal critics often show poor literary judgment. Reading the Bible is not enough: one needs "wide and deep and genial experience of literature in general" to recognize what makes the gospels special. But many critics miss what stands out about the stories of Jesus. For example, Bultmann called the Gospel of John "vision literature," and compared it to John Bunyan's *Pilgrim's Progress*. Lewis replied:

"I have been reading poems, romances, vision-literature, legend, myth, all my life. I know what they are like. I know that not one of them is like this."

Lewis was especially dumbfounded by Bultmann's claim that the gospels do not preserve a "personality" of Jesus. "Through what strange process has this learned German gone in order to make himself blind to what all men except him see?" "They lack literary judgement," Lewis said of the Trumpkins of his day: "They claim to see fern-seed and can't see an elephant ten yards away in broad daylight."

Second, many "brilliant" theories about who Jesus "really" was (a cottage industry that has continued to grow after Lewis' passing) assume that modern scholars can see Jesus more clearly than people who lived within his culture, spoke his language, and shared common assumptions about life. Having immersed himself in classical and medieval worlds from childhood, Lewis found the arrogance and "chronological snobbery" of such critics ridiculous. Uncle Andrew may be better-educated than a guinea pig, but the guinea pig inhabits the Wood Between the Worlds, and knows it is grassy. So much more, a first century Palestinian would have understood a thousand things about her own culture that a twenty-first century PhD in Near Middle Eastern Studies can only guess at. The modern PhD (still more, Internet surfer) should approach such distant texts with due humility.

Third, many critics assumed, Lewis noted, that miracles can't happen. Indeed. Ernest Renan said the gospels must in part be legendary, because they're "full of miracles." David Strauss said "we can only accept the natural" in them. More recent scholars, like E. P. Sanders and co-founders of the Jesus Seminar, also analyze the gospels from materialistic premises. In *Honest to Jesus,* Robert Funk called miracles an "affront to common sense" that should make us "snicker." In his "revolutionary biography" of Jesus, John Crossan wrote, "I do not think that anyone, anywhere, at any time brings dead people back to life."

But one must distinguish between (a) historical evidence and (b) careful thinking about what is possible. A New Testament scholar may know (a) without having any expertise in (b). And one needs to fairly engage contrary arguments. Lewis was a philosopher as well as a literary scholar, and wrote a book defending the possibility of miracles.

More recently, New Testament scholar Craig Keener wrote an 1140-page book describing reports of modern miracles, some of which he or family members claimed to have experienced. Part II of that work, pages 83-208, is entitled "Are Miracles Possible?" In it he engages the arguments of thinkers like David Hume against miracles. Similarly, while philosophers Timothy and Lydia McGrew are well-known for their ground-breaking historical arguments for the gospels, Tim is also author of the entry on "Miracles" for the *Stanford Encyclopedia of Philosophy*, dealing with philosophical doubts there. Even members of the Jesus Seminar Walter Wink and Marcus Borg found reason to think there may be more to life than is dreamt of in Robert Funk's philosophy.

While Lewis might have admitted that Keener, McGrew, or Wink have better reason to believe in miracles than Bultmann or Funk to deny them, he did not naively claim, "seeing is believing." Uncle Andrew saw, and did not believe. Jadis believed, but without saving faith. The crew of the Dawn Treader heard scissors and gongs, and saw things settle on the mast or crawl up the sides of the ship. But Lucy rightly took those sensual experiences as dreams or hallucinations.

We'll dig more deeply into this crucial question of miracles in a later chapter. Lewis' point was, New Testament scholars should not dismiss such claims on unexamined philosophical grounds, as they often do.

Finally, Lewis noted that modern scholars often offer "informed" guesses about how, when and why the gospels were written. Because they are well-read and intelligent, their guesses convince many. (Ehrman is the present reigning champion on this tour.) Book reviewers often also reconstruct how the works they analyze came to be written. But as a best-selling author himself, with countless writer friends, Lewis knew the actual origin of many books reviewed, and found such guesses consistently wrong.

Many claimed, for example, that the ring in J. R. R. Tolkien's *Lord of the Rings* symbolized the atomic bomb. This sounds quite plausible. The bomb, like the ring, is a small manufactured object with enormous destructive power. During World War II, three great powers, two totalitarian, one free (like Mordor, Isengard, and

Gondor), struggled to gain this "ring of power." The "good guys" got it first, and were tempted to use it.

The parallels seem clear and convincing. Only Lewis, who had coaxed Tolkien into finishing "the new Hobbit" (as they called it), knew this origin story was untrue. The ring emerged long before Tolkien heard of the bomb. Indeed, in a letter to his son Christopher in August, 1945, Tolkien expressed shock: "The news today about 'atomic bombs' is so horrifying one is stunned." But in May of the previous year, Tolkien wrote the same son that he had just read the chapter, "The Choices of Master Samwise," to Lewis, who was "affected to tears," encouraging Tolkien to go on! That chapter comes near the end of *Lord of the Rings*, when the One Ring had been central to the story for hundreds of pages. So yes, ring long before (news of) bomb.

Another example of how modern critics who know the language and culture still guess wrong, involves Aslan himself. Lewis' good friend the writer Roger Lancelot Green, with whom he would travel to Greece, had written a story about a tiger. Lewis wrote about a lion. It was natural to suppose one borrowed from or had been deeply influenced by the other. In fact, Lewis said, the two cats were unrelated. He concluded: "My impression is that in the whole of my experience not one of these guesses has on any one point been right. I can't remember a single hit."

If modern reviewers, who know the language, culture, and thought patterns of the writers they review, so consistently guess wrong about the origin of ideas, why trust similar guesses about how the gospels were penned 2000 years ago?

Many insightful men and women have contributed to New Testament studies, and perhaps Lewis was too dismissive. N. T. Wright, an Anglican bishop whom Raymond Martin called "far and away the most sophisticated and articulate philosopher of historical methodology" in the field, thought Lewis had much to learn from New Testament scholars. I have learned even from radical skeptics, like the eccentric Jesus mythicists Robert Price and Richard Carrier (both of whom I have debated). But Lewis knew literature far better than any New Testament scholar I have encountered. And recent waves of Jesus criticism show that a scholar may dream in Aramaic and Hebrew, yet remain deaf as Uncle Andrew to the Voice of Aslan.

The gospels are shocking documents. Lewis thought their closest parallels were James Boswell's portrait of his friend Samuel Johnson, or Plato's picture of his teacher Socrates. I also find parallels in the *Analects* of Confucius, another collection of stories and sayings gathered by a kindly teacher's disciples soon after his passing.

But often, like Lewis, I get the impression that critics overlook facts standing before their eyes big as an elephant (or lion). Other skeptics remind me of Trumpkin, clambering down cliffs after shadows they strain to see.

"Wraiths and Wreckage:" Scholars Befriend Aslan

In his biography of Jesus, A. N. Wilson seemed to see a shadow pacing before him in the queer evening light:

> The realistic details are too many, and too odd, for me to be able to accept that they were all invented by some unsung novelistic genius of the first century…That is John's great paradox. The more he piles artifice upon artifice, trope upon trope, the more real his pictures become, to the point where it becomes almost impossible not to believe that some such conversation, with a Samaritan woman, must have taken place.

Perhaps because of those "realistic details," Wilson eventually returned to Christian faith. This is what earlier drew Lewis to

Christ: the gospels combine clear signs of historicity with mythical "tropes."

Lewis taught philosophy as a young man, when his own views were still in flux. One day a fellow teacher, whom he described as "the toughest of the tough," "the hardest boiled of all the atheists I ever knew," probably Thomas Weldon, with whom Lewis shared philosophy tutoring duties, visited his office in Magdalen College and dropped a bombshell. He said the evidence for the historicity of the gospels was excellent. "'Rum thing,' he went on. 'All that stuff of Frazer's about the Dying God. Rum thing. It almost looks as if it had really happened once.'"

Weldon was indeed "tough." He rose to the rank of captain in Field Artillery in World War I, winning the Military Cross and Bar, awarded for "an act or acts of exemplary gallantry during active operations against the enemy on land." While the young Lewis described him as a "sinister presence" in a letter to his father, Weldon seemed to enjoy the role of gadfly. Another colleague called him a "past master" at the art of arguing undergraduates out of their beliefs, then arguing them out of their new radicalism, "leaving them mystified as to what they believed and suspended in a free-floating state of cleverness."

I imagine C. S. Lewis would be delighted by the surge of serious study of Christian origins by scholars who do not casually dismiss miracles, who listen to original sources with due humility, and whose cleverness, rather than floating freely, binds to facts.

I have written three books on the historical Jesus myself. In the first, I describe a dozen errors that skeptics often commit in reading the gospels, including the four Lewis pointed out. In the second, I show that eminent scholars like Elaine Pagels, Karen King, and Bart Ehrman overlook obvious facts about gnostic works that they compare to the stories of Jesus. (Draping lion skins over donkeys.) In the third, I shine critical light on popular, and often asinine, "fake Aslans" of Historical Jesus studies. Following New Testament scholars and astute observers like Lewis, Chesterton, Pascal, and M. Scott Peck, I develop a set of thirty markers of historical truth, that show from many angles that the gospels can be trusted.

But maybe Susan, who met the lion, then decided to "grow up" and move on, is the person to question such claims. Perhaps she ultimately sought another portal to Aslan's Country from our world, the doorway that Thomas and Trumpkin had once knocked on, called "doubt."

"Once a friend of Narnia, always a friend of Narnia." Susan did not die in the tragic rail accident described in *The Last Battle*. I imagine it shook her deeply, though. She may have raged against God when she lost her whole family in one horrible day. Maybe she tried to numb her senses with wild living for a while.

Susan had been allowed into Narnia as a child, so she could learn to know Aslan "by another name" in our world. Perhaps in time, she found herself kneeling on the ground, like Shasta, to examine marks made by the passage of one whose voice had long ago spoken to her out of the fog. ("You have listened to fears, child.") Maybe she picked up the gospels, read the "experts" who study them, then took her questions to an older man she had long trusted: a scholar with peculiar experiences of his own and a passion for sound reasoning, who (it turns out) also avoided that fatal train.

Recommended Reading

Basic: On Jesus, of course begin with the gospels! Josh McDowell's *More Than a Carpenter*, Lee Strobel's *The Case for Christ*, John

Ortberg's *Who is This Man?*, and John Stott's *The Incomparable Christ*, offer good second-hand introductions. For background on the story about Susan in the next chapter, read *The Last Battle*.

Advanced: Of my own books on the historical Jesus, I most strongly recommend *Jesus is No Myth: The Fingerprints of God on the Gospels*. (Though you will have to endure some typos in the present print version, unfortunately.) I also recommend Craig Blomberg's *The Historical Reliability of the Gospels* and *The Historical Reliability of the New Testament*, and the first two volumes in N. T. Wright's *Christian Origins and the Question of God* series. Craig Keener and Ben Witherington provide rewarding and helpful reading on the Book of Acts. You may like to read skeptics like Borg, Bultmann, Crossan, Ehrman, Funk, Sanders, and Vermes. Like "Fernseed and Elephants," my books on this subject explain why I don't think such skeptics introduce the "real Aslan." But one can find many nuggets of truth in their work: Borg's *Meeting Jesus Again for the First Time* reminds me of Trumpkin or Shasta fumbling in the fog, while other classics of skeptic Jesus Studies could have been written by Uncle Andrew. In this chapter, I also cite Raymond Martin's *The Elusive Messiah: A Philosophical Overview of the Quest for the Historical Jesus*, and Walter Wink's *Engaging the Powers*.

Aside from the article on miracles by Timothy McGrew, and Hume himself, "On Miracles," I also recommend John Earman, *Hume's Abject Failure: The Argument Against Miracles*. Also cited in this chapter is A. N. Wilson's *Jesus: A Life*, which may be even shakier than his bio of Lewis, but contains good nuggets. Thomas Waldon is mentioned by R. W. Johnson in a 1999 review of a book by Niall Ferguson, in the *London Review of Books*.

FIVE

Susan Comes Calling

Scene: A second-floor office in a functional stone building, with windows overlooking a grassy quadrangle and ornate spires. An elderly man is staring into space, books jumbled in lopsided piles on his desk. A drawing hangs near the door, of two men in old-fashioned wigs, sitting in a wooden boat with feathered wings, flying above the very quad visible out the window. One is smoking a pipe, while the other trails fishing tackle, at which peck a flock of ducks. A basket of apples rests on the cupboard below the drawing: a faint humming sound can be heard from the cupboard.

Knock, knock!

"Come in!"

A young lady of about twenty-five enters. She is stylishly-dressed and attractive, with long black hair and a skirt to match. She smiles, a bit crookedly, as if some weight were pressing on her cheeks.

The old man looks up, and his mouth drops open.

"My dear! So good to see you!"

"Sorry, professor ... It's been ... a while."

"Sit down, sit down! Tea? Coffee?"

"Tea, if it's not too much trouble!"

"I have been praying for you."

"Does it hit the ceiling and bounce back?"

The old man glances at his guest with furrowed brows. He nips several tea leaves and drops them in a ceramic mug decorated with a picture of a cat prowling among peonies.

"Here you are," the professor sighs. The girl puts her hand on his shoulder.

"Sorry, Uncle Digs. But I do wonder. Am I a total lunatic? Did all that— really happen?"

"Crazy? No. But you do look tired. What have you been up to for the past, what is it, four years?"

"Searching for a door back in, I guess. But it seems the Emperor needed my parents beyond the bloody sea more than their daughter did!"

"I am so sorry. If there is anything I can do— anything at all."

"Well, I wouldn't mind some sugar. And a few answers, if you can spare them, Professor."

"Even if all those crazy memories were real— horseback rides with centaurs, visits from princes— Rabadash was a dish, you know, I would have loved to see him in donkey ears— the funny way Tumnus danced out of rooms after he scored a diplomatic victory— I can't believe I'm saying these things out loud to another human being— how would I prove it? Or maybe there's another way in. Maybe if I could find some clue that Aslan came to our world, I would feel a tad less ... alone.

"So I started visiting the Bod."

"To find ...?"

"If our Aslan is real. I mean, hang it all, half the colleges in this town— Jesus, Christ Church, Body of Christ ... hang his name over their entryways."

"Magdalen for a pert lady disciple."

"Yes. And a bunch are named for male apostles, too. So I started reading Bultmann. Crossan. Vermes. Meier. Pagels. Ehrman.

Piles of stuff, and everyone seemed to find a different Jesus, like the blind men and the elephant."

"But who did you find?"

"If you don't mind, professor, let me ask the questions. Sorry. I guess that means, I haven't made up my mind. Except I think Empress Jadis runs this hell-hole of a planet." She smiled faintly. "Especially London. London is the worst."

"When a man is tired of London, he is tired of life," the professor thought to himself. Still, her sarcasm showed spirit. That had to be a good sign.

"I will answer any questions I can. But the older I get, my dear, the more befuddled I become."

The girl set her tea down and looked around the room. She spied the drawing of the men in the flying boat.

"Your drinking mates? Is that a keg of gun powder next to the chap in back who is smoking? ... looks like a young Einstein, with that bald pate."

"Indeed! Hair lent Samson physical strength. But baldness lends those of us so fortunate as to possess it rare intellectual powers!" The professor laughed. "A friend upstairs sketched that. John Wilkins and Robert Hooke traveling to the moon. The scientific revolution more or less began in this college, don't you know? As I read it, this means that imagination must precede science or technology. Aristotle was a student of Plato. Without vision, even scientists perish. So Einstein isn't in this vehicle—he was too young—but he would have been sympathetic with the artist's 'flight of imagination,' if you will."

"Speaking of imagination, professor. A little girl comes into your office in that drafty old Victorian monster of a house— why did you have to sell it?— tells you she's hopped into another world through your closet. And you, a world-renowned 'critical scholar,' say you believe her? What did you see that more respectable scholars overlook?"

The old man drummed his fingers on his desk.

"Peter asked me, 'How could there be other worlds, just around the corner?' I had jumped in those puddles, you see. But I was also thinking of conversations with members of the physics faculty in this very room. It seems belief in many worlds has become fashionable again, don't you know?

"I'll give you my reasons. Mind you, anyone outside this room would be mad to believe them. But madness, too, seems the fashion now, and they may help you in your quest."

"Do you have time?"

"Class begins in half an hour. Tell you what. First, I'll explain why I believed Lucy, and your story about Aslan. Then, if we can meet for lunch after noon— is the Mitre OK?— I'll explain about that other Aslan."

"It's a date!"

"I had, or came to have, several reasons for believing Lucy's story. First, she was obviously not joking, or telling a tale for fun. You and Peter wouldn't have come to me in the first place if you weren't convinced she was serious."

"That's not much to go on."

"Second, she told a story. Stories are easier to remember than a series of propositions or abstract arguments, especially for a little girl.

"Like Goldilocks and the Three Bears?" the woman answered doubtfully.

"We begin with the simple and obvious. In history, there is no question of proof— we seek to learn what is most likely. Third, Lucy stuck to her story even though it inconvenienced her. She loved you, and frankly, she worshiped the ground Peter walked on.

She didn't want you to think poorly of her. All she had to do was say, 'Sorry, I was joking.' But she stuck with her story for weeks. That's pretty impressive for a child her age."

"That's what, in Historical Jesus studies, they call the 'Criterion of Embarrassment,' right?

"Yes. There are all kinds of things in the gospels that would have embarrassed later Christians, like Peter's denial, and Jesus' cry from the cross, 'My God, why have you forsaken me.'"

"But some critics say you can never prove what a later writer might have found embarrassing. Maybe Mark wanted to make Peter look foolish, say because his faction was competing for power with Peter's faction in the early Church. When Aslan confessed his fears to us, that only made him love him more, anyway."

"Read the Stoics, my dear. They idolized Socrates, how he calmly drank the hemlock— have some more tea, Susie? I promise I won't poison you— that was how heroes died. But here Jesus is, letting a prostitute wash his feet with her hair, weeping over his friend's death, and crying out that God had abandoned him on the cross!"

"I know that feeling!"

"I expect you do. But that didn't fit the heroic 'tough guy' image of the day. Even Stephen died a martyr's death without complaint! Pascal wondered, what inventor of Messiahs would make the Son of God more vulnerable and 'weak' than one of his own disciples? Aslan is 'true beast' because he does not disguise his weakness. Like Jesus in the Garden, he begged for your company when he walked up the hill to the Stone Table."

"I remember. 'I am sad and lonely,' he said. But what is your point? That Jesus wasn't the kind of hero ancient people invented? That seems a little subjective. There was probably a market for a variety of preferences in personality." The young woman set her tea on the table. "But go on."

"Fourth, Lucy didn't have time to forget: only a few moments had passed."

"How does that help the gospels, professor? Some scholars say they were written 'generations' after the events they describe, after the earliest witnesses had all died off. Then the stories were passed down from one person and culture to another— Jews to Greeks to Latins and Goths— by 'Chinese whispers,' Ehrman calls it, with witnesses garbling the facts more with each transmission."

The professor smiled. "Some New Testament scholars seem to be even worse at math than I am! Actually most scholars agree that the gospels were written beginning about thirty or forty years after the events they recorded. That trip I took with Aunt Polly was sixty-two years ago this summer. Do you think I can forget it, even for a day? At your age, you have no idea how common old memories will one day become."

"But people died so young in the ancient world!

"Not always. Socrates and Confucius made it past seventy. Many early scientists survived into their sixties, seventies, even eighties—Hippocrates, Aristotle, Theophrastus, Archimedes, Strato of Lampsacus. The death rate was higher largely because of infant mortality, and partly because of the ruthlessness of the Romans. But if you survived infancy, and dodged the legions, you could put in some good innings. If the ancients died out as quickly as some modern scholars suppose, none of us would be here! Those fantastic death rates just don't tally.

"Plus, Jesus' disciples would have been younger than him, in their twenties or teens. Mobile revolutionary movements are usually full of young men— though maybe not as young as the four of you were, when you overthrew Jadis VIII of Charn."

"I'll take credit for that, if you give it to me!" The young woman smiled and held out her hands, as if to receive a prize. Her host smiled, and shook his head slowly.

"And we know the 'Chinese whispers' theory is false. When you came back through the wardrobe, you remembered some proper names: Aslan, Narnia, Jadis. I knew those names. Get some friends together and toss Korean or Latvian names into a game of Telephone Tag. Sometimes I experiment like that on my students— doubtless the Uncle Andrew in me. Try it out, and I guarantee that foreign names will be the first thing your friends will garble. So the fact that Lucy remembered those names— names I knew, and never talked about to anyone but Aunt Polly, whom you didn't know at the time— confirmed the story to me."

"How does that apply to the 'Aslan of Oxford?'"

The professor picked up a thick paperback with a crude early Medieval drawing of men around a table on the cover, one of whom was crowned by a halo. "Jesus and the Eyewitnesses."

"Take this! Read chapter— Let's see— Chapter Four! See these charts? You know the names: Simeon, Joseph, Lazarus, Judas, Jesus, Ananias— then over here: Mary, Salome, Martha, Joanna, Sapphira…Dr. Bauckham shows that the names reported in the gospels, male and female, and even their frequencies, closely match the frequency of the same names found in tombs in First Century Palestine. If these stories had been passed from generation to generation, and across cultures, as Ehrman claims, they would have become garbled, as in Telephone Tag. You would not get such consistently close matches. This proves that the authors of the gospels were close enough to the facts to get even minute details right."

The young woman raised a finger. "But if Matthew or Luke wanted to make the story sound plausible, wouldn't they do a little research on the culture they were writing about?" Her host stood up and tapped his finger on an even thicker, black book. The girl turned her head sideways and read, "Collected Ancient Greek Novels."

"We know that in fact ancient novelists didn't— probably couldn't—go to the trouble of the detailed cross-cultural research that would be required. Anyway, this shows that the theory of 'Chinese Whispers' is incredible. These four authors did not, in fact, garble minor, culturally-related facts, as the theory demands."

The girl squinted, as if pondering the matter.

"Fifth, there is the fact that ultimately, all four of you agreed about Narnia— four largely independent attestations, like four gospels, make the story vastly more likely."

"But maybe Lucy talked us into playing a trick on you! And scholars say Luke, Matthew, and John copied from St. Mark!"

"Good point! Stories have to be truly independent, to confirm one another. But when basic facts agree, while details differ— that is what the police look for at a crime scene. Eyewitnesses tend to notice different details. The same is true of ancient history. Accounts of the lives of Socrates or Alexander differ in detail, but generally cohere on central points. That is the pattern historians look for to establish accuracy, and it's pretty much what we find in the gospels. There is some overlap, but each writer also brings unique materials. There may actually be more than four sources agreeing on the passion, for instance."

"Hold on, Uncle! I didn't ask why you believed all four of us after we came back! I asked why you believed Lucy!"

The sun poked out, shining on the basket of apples. The old man noticed his guest glancing that way, grabbed a knife from a drawer, and cut an apple up. His guest took several slices. She noticed the humming sound, stared at the cupboard, then grinned at her host, as if at a wicked fellow-conspirator.

"I never told you the whole story," he went on, raising an eyebrow. "But I knew that wardrobe. My sixth reason to believe Lucy is that her story fit my own childhood memories: not just names, but the very feel of the place she described. This is what historians call the 'Criterion of Coherence.'

"Lots of children tell stories about talking animals.

"But not stories that fit my experiences as a child, including her report that the land behind the Wardrobe was ruled by a talking lion! And there were also a couple of what you might call... " The old man plucked another volume off his desk... "What these two Americans call 'Undesigned Coincidences.'"

"'Unresigned commissions?' What, a washed up colonel who won't leave his barracks?

"*Unde*signed co*incidences*. Odd little details in your story, that matched odd little details in mine."

"Such as?"

"Such as the light in the woods."

"The what?"

"The lantern. I saw the thing planted and grow."

"Lanterns don't grow, professor," the woman responded, reaching for another apple. "You make me feel better though— you're even battier than I am!" She laughed. "These apples are exquisite! But why shouldn't someone put a lantern in two different stories? I imagine light has some deep, dark Jungian meaning..."

"That's just it. If these were stories in two different books by the same author, yes, I'd say he probably made it up. But I'm talking about a minor detail in your story, and how it cohered with a minor detail in mine. No one outside this office has any reason to believe it. But within this room, when the experiences of two different individuals match, we do. Or at least I thought I did."

"How does this 'undersigned coherence' apply to Jesus?"

"*Undesigned coincidences.* This McGrew lady shows that the gospels, and other New Testament books, are loaded with little coincidences that fit together."

"So the fabulous *femme fatale* Susan Pevensie and the great Professor Digory Kirke might be nutty as fruitcakes, but not Matthew, Mark, Luke or John?"

"You and I might just be figures in a children's story, for all the greater world knows. And here's another point. I took Lucy in for questioning."

"What? You told us to mind our own business!"

"Yes. But I felt responsible...All right, and was dying of curiosity. Lucy described Tumnus' house to me, and even gave me the titles of a couple books on the faun's bookshelf. 'The Life and Letters of Silenus.' 'Men, Monks and Gamekeepers; a Study in Popular Legend or Is Man a Myth.' Does that sound like the sort of thing a nine-year-old would make up?"

"She was ten by then. And she might have seen those books somewhere. And what does that have to do with Jesus?"

"What strikes me, when I read the gospels, is how commonplace, yet realistic, the words of most characters in them are, including the narrators. The words of Jesus extrude from that matrix, far more than those book titles transcend a nine— sorry, ten-year-old's concept of anthropology. I cannot believe that Mark, or even Luke or John, invented Jesus. He is vastly beyond them."

The professor stared out the window. Clouds were moving in from the south, and the sunlight was fading. He put on a pair of glasses and looked at his young visitor again. She appeared with the kind of double vision with which the old sometimes see young people they have watched grow up, as if Ben Franklin's bifocals resolved people into two different ages.

"You came back talking about 'deep magic before the dawn of time,' and translating Christian theology into, 'When a willing victim who had committed no treachery was killed in a traitor's stead, the Table would crack and Death itself would stark working backwards.' Do you know any thirteen-year-old girls who talk that way?"

"I bet you could do it, professor!" his visitor answered with a twinkle in her eye.

"Perhaps I could. Come of reading Plato."

They both laughed. Susan glanced at the clock, and gestured to the professor to continue.

"Lucy's strange words were a specimen of what Mircea Eliade called mythological language from 'outside of time.' But the language of Jesus is beyond his biographers in too many ways to explain over one cup of tea. Homer, Virgil, Shakespeare, Milton, Dickens— traditionally, great writers tended to distribute their brilliance into the mouths of many speakers. The pompous Polonius gives a speech to his son we still quote 400 years later: 'To thine own self be true.' A gravedigger is full of dark wit and wisdom. A hero on the field before Troy breaks into a long poetic speech in the heat of battle. Most writers, if they had it, flaunted it. Or they turned minor characters into a 'Greek Chorus,' echoing the mood of the moment, to focus attention on the heroes— that was common in Greek plays and novels."

"Whereas our Aslan . . . ?"

"The gospels are almost in a class by themselves, in that and in many other ways. Minor characters are undeniably realistic: Pharisees jealous and skeptical, crowds sometimes with Jesus and sometimes against him, disciples meaning well, but vacillating, competitive, and weak. Against that we meet several vivid, realistic sketches like the man born blind, or the woman with the vase full of perfume. We get to know Peter best among the disciples: to a teacher, a tellingly realistic touch: there's usually one loudmouth to a class. But above these characters rises, like the Matterhorn above foothills, a personality who never answers a straight question directly, who expresses feelings in a most un-Stoic manner, who speaks the greatest lines ever, and treats those around him, especially women, in an utterly revolutionary manner."

The professor paused for a moment, and hearing no objections, went on.

"Suppose I tried telling our story about a talking lion to anyone outside this office –say, my skeptical chemistry colleague down the hall. All the arguments for Narnia I just gave would collapse.

"Aslan has no multiple attestation. All the stories would come from one old professor whom everyone knows likes the philosophical tales of Plato. These are stories which, with a little thought, I might make up. The hard part would be for me to invent you young people, but everyone knows some children stayed at my house during the war. I might invent the words of Aslan, which sound suspiciously like those of Jesus, anyway. We know why: because he's the same person! But my friends would find another explanation: I read the gospels, then wrote this lion character to sound like Jesus."

The professor noticed his young friend was staring out the window, and halted. A little bird with a black head and yellow breast hopped along the windowsill, grabbed a crumb of food, and flew to a tree about thirty feet away.

"Really, professor? Aslan is kind to women? 'How much more does your Father in heaven value you than many sparrows!' Do you know what that telegram did? Dad! Mom! Little Lu, Pete and Ed! Tory blames Labor. Labor blames Big Coal. Whom should I blame? God? Myself, for not being on the train with them?"

The professor set down his tea, and grasped the young woman's hand with both of his.

"Winter lasts long, my dear. I know. And unfortunately, my morning class is waiting. But you are never forgotten. Please, meet me ten minutes before noon, on the third floor of the Mitre. My treat."

"All right. Let's see if Aslan turns up. Or bring me a couple of those rings in your cupboard."

The professor started. His students always assumed that sound was of a cell phone charging. Susan had grown into a sharp young lady, indeed.

II. Facing window seats at the Mitre. The clock had tolled Noon some time before. The window looks out on High Street, where people pass with umbrellas over shiny cobblestones.

"Sorry I'm late, professor."

"Quite all right. I took the liberty of dining first. I have a meeting at two. Do try the salmon!"

"Maybe just a scone and some coffee."

"Whatever you like. Was I any help this morning?"

"Sorry if I was a bit nervy. Meeting you brought back so many memories...You say that the gospels can be believed, because...let's see...they are early, and four of them mostly agree. They tell a story, which are easier to remember, and they claim to be telling what really happened. The names they record neatly fit names from tombstones in early Palestine. The stories they tell are embarrassing..."

"They contain numerous elements that a pious believer would be highly unlikely to invent."

"Yes. And you said Jesus didn't act like ancient heroes were expected to act. He was too kind to women, for one thing, and too honest in his emotions. Plus something about coherence and coincidences. I think I get that. It's like finding my dog's paw prints by the chair where I left the chicken panini, with the lettuce and onion on the floor and the rest gone. The simplest explanation that covers all the facts is usually best."

"Yes, that is part of it. The story of Jesus comes to us from several sources— whether you count the gospels themselves, or 'Q' and materials peculiar to Luke and Matthew. While there is some debate about genre, roughly speaking, they take the form of *bioi* or Greek biography, not of novel, epic or play or any other known form of fiction. And did I say, unlike most Sumerian or Greek fiction, they talk about a carpenter and fishermen, rather than a god or king?"

"I don't think you mentioned that. Why does it matter?"

"It has to do with the embarrassing realism of the gospels. Unlike the Gnostic Jesus, the 'real Aslan' asks questions to learn answers. He thirsts, cries, feels frustrated and abandoned."

"While Aslan comes and goes— 'not a tame lion,' and all that?"

"More or less. There are a bunch of qualities that make the gospels fantastically credible, to which Aslan provides no parallels. Evidence I could mention to my colleagues without being laughed out of the room."

"OK, professor. Mind if I take notes?" Susan opened her purse and took out a pad and pen.

"Unlike Narnia, the places described in the gospels are recognized locations: you can visit the Mount of Olives, the Sea of Galilee, the town of Jesus' birth, the sea he is said to have calmed, the site of a synagogue in which he preached ... "

"There seems to be some debate over how accurate those references are."

"Scholars used to say that John couldn't have known the city of Jerusalem, because he talked about an imaginary Pool of Bethesda with five porticoes— but then the place was excavated. A chap named Colin Hemer describes eighty-four specific facts that can be verified in the last seventeen or so chapters of the *Book of Acts*: locations, landmarks, gods worshiped, dialects, local industries, the altar to the unknown god…Clearly, Luke was a careful historian. By contrast, Narnia doesn't fit into any complex body of independent historical, geographical and archaeological data. It is 'off the grid,' as they say."

"It would be hard to get a grant to do a dig in the ruins of Care Paravel."

"Precisely! Well, dig into your pastry! I brought you another book, don't worry if you get strawberry jam on it."

"Raspberry."

"The author is Tom Wright. He describes a quality in the gospels that he calls 'double similarity, double dissimilarity.' The point is these old stories are both like and unlike their parent and daughter faiths: Jewish religious tradition, and the Christian Church. Jesus is Jewish to the bone. Hundreds of filaments connect his life and teaching to Hebrew thought and experience. Yet no Jew ever dared say or do the sorts of things Jesus did. He subverted his own traditions."

Professor Kirke tapped his watch.

"It is as if some engineering genius lost in the desert took this apart, filed and twisted and bent its parts, then turned them into a cell phone and called 999 for help. Jesus is Jewish— you can't explain him outside of that. But he does something to Jewish tradition that is unique and astonishingly inventive."

"Maybe Jewish Christians added that Messianic stuff later?"

"But his relationship with the Church is similarly complex. The gospels make sense as the foundation of Christianity. They explain where the new faith came from. But the Church does not explain them. No believer spoke with the authority and sheer eccentricity of Jesus. Church fathers cite the *Sermon on the Mount* and Jesus' parables, but you will not find their like among later saints, even when the Church developed a stable of talented writers."

"But wasn't the early church mostly slaves and other marginalized persons?"

"That is a common myth. New religious movements are usually established at least in large part among the elite, and Christianity was no exception."

"Uncle Digs. If you were writing the gospels, could you have invented that story?"

"Not a chance. Nor could any of the Nobel Prize winning book worms in this city. Jesus ranks with Kafka or Zhuang Zi merely as a teller of parables. But his stories touch the heart and speak to the needs of listeners far more deeply."

The professor waved his hand at shelves to his left marked "World Literature."

"Dickens called 'The Prodigal Son' the most perfect story in literature. Pascal, whom Voltaire recognized as one of the greatest French stylists, wrote, 'Jesus Christ said great things so simply that it seems as though He had not thought them great; and yet so clearly that we easily see what He thought of them. This clearness, joined to this simplicity, is wonderful.' Tolstoy, the greatest novelist of all, was dumbfounded by the Sermon on the Mount. Gandhi and Martin Luther King borrowed bits of it to dramatically reform India and America.

"And such words, like bombs that create instead of blasting cities to pieces, were invented by some anonymous First Century apologist? Or several independently? Impossible!"

"So Jesus was really, really clever. Does that mean he could walk on water? Or escort me back to Narnia?"

"It's not just that Jesus was good with words, it's that his words introduce new elements into the human story. Genesis begins with that great line, 'In the Beginning, God created the heavens and the earth.' John's version is, 'In the beginning was the Word, and the

Word was God...and the Word became flesh, and dwelt among us...' How could even the greatest reformer or scientist live up to such an introduction? Yet Jesus does so easily. His words have terra-formed the human heart for new life. If I were hard-nosed atheist, I could still not deny the impact of this second Song of Creation."

"Seems a little abstract...Can you be more concrete?"

"For instance, Jesus noticed people in pain. He praised those whom others despised— widows, adulteresses, tax collectors, for-eigners. But he never flattered them. At the same time, he often read the powerful the riot act."

The professor lowered his voice, as a diner at a neighboring table glanced at him.

"Read Homer and Virgil. Dip into that pompous windbag, *Apollonius of Tyana*, whom many of those scholars you have been reading foolishly compare to Jesus. Read the ancient historians: Arrian, Plutarch, Caesar, or best of all Suetonius. He describes how a common emperor, not a particularly crazy one, crowded the edge of the Coliseum to catch blood spatter from the 'games.' The average Roman male made British football hooligans look like Luna Lovegood.

"How strange, in such an utterly ruthless culture, to see how Jesus noticed nobodies on the side of the road. He treated wom-en with a dignity, compassion, and respect that remains shocking in the Me-Too era, but was mind-boggling in the Greco-Roman world."

Susan thought of Queen Jadis' knife. Why did every church in England raise a cross to heaven, as if to remind God of bad human habits like torture and oppression?

"You may think this an odd question from me, professor. But some people say miracles are the 'least-likely' explanation for any event. They say any explanation is superior. After all, when you look into stories of ghosts, fairies, miracles, visitations, they turn out to be hoaxes, or some silly cop who sees a light over a power station and thinks he's spotted a UFO.

"So why should anyone believe our story? Or the story the ancient evangelists tell about Jesus? Doesn't the sheer improbability of miracles outweigh Unsigned Collaboration or whatever you call it, and all those other historical fingerprints you describe?"

Dr. Kirke lit his pipe, leaned back in his chair, and glanced out the window. It was raining hard now, and pedestrians were huddled beneath the clock of Carfax Tower.

"I saw Narnia created out of dirt and darkness. Maybe old Davy Hume just didn't get out enough. Your friend Eustace might have talked sense into him— after he dedragoned."

Susan laughed. "What a pill that brat used to be! We would have paid Jill to throw him off the cliff!"

"Look, Susan. You can never persuade scoffers. You wanted to know if your childhood memories correspond to anything that can be shown to be real in this world. I hope I have helped a little, and the books I lent you will help more. The gospels are, in fact, covered with divine fingerprints, with subtle evidences that they are truthful historical sources. Let's talk about miracles another day. How was your scone?"

"OK, professor. Not as good as your apples. Have you been sneaking off to London and stealing fruit— or rings? Oh, and speaking of miracles, did you know I'm dating again?"

"I can't imagine what young man could possibly deserve you!"

"Don't be silly, Uncle Digs. Might I pop in with him, some day? I may have questions after reading your books."

"My dear, the door into my world will always be open to you and any friend— but please, not another Rabadash. Lucy told me all about him."

Further Reading

Beginning: *For the next chapter, please read* Voyage of the Dawn Treader *and* Silver Chair.

Advanced: *Aside from the books recommended at the end of the last chapter, Professor Kirke also mentions Richard Bauckham's excellent* Jesus and the Eyewitnesses. *Also mentioned is Mircea Eliade, see* The Myth of the Eternal Return. *Colin Hemer's* The Book of Acts in the Setting of Hellenistic History *gives the list of verified claims in Acts. For Gandhi's use of the teachings of Jesus, see his* Autobiography. *Tim McGrew's article on miracles is searchable online. British philosopher Stephen Law, author of* Believing Bullshit, *mentions the police officers who saw UFOs. We debated the issue on his website, and at Christthetao.blogspot.com.*

My Jesus is No Myth: the Fingerprints of God on the Gospels *covers much of the ground of the last two chapters in depth.*

SIX

A Different Sort of Magic

"Ever since the song began, she felt that this whole world was filled with a Magic different from hers and stronger. She hated it. She would have smashed that world, or all worlds, to pieces, if it would only stop the singing." The Magician's Nephew

The Empress Jadis came to Narnia just in time to witness its creation. The lion sang the world's heavenly bodies and living organisms into being. Jadis recognized the power of Aslan's song, being practiced in magic herself. But she perceived his power as a threat, because it was stronger and "different from hers." She liked to rule worlds, and he was clearly a barrier to power. Worse, Aslan's song got under her skin. Perhaps she felt intuitively that her magic was out of tune to the song of her own original creation.

Uncle Andrew, meanwhile, refused to believe that lions could sing or talk.

Christian miracles, which Susan asked about in the previous chapter, are denied for all those reasons.

Some say Nature is all that is. Miracles cannot occur because there is no one to work them. A miracle, according to David Hume, is a "violation" of the course of Nature. (A word often used as a synonym for "rape.") People tell tales about fairies, ghosts, gods, spaghetti monsters, and tea cups that orbit the Earth. Examine those stories carefully, and there always turns out to be a good non-supernatural explanation: lie, dream, hallucination, wishful thinking, literary fantasy, too many bottles of beer or hits of LSD off the wall, or a long chain of careless oral transmissions ("Chinese Whispers").

In fact, as Susan vaguely remembered, Hume said miracles must be the least likely explanation for an event. If you find a cookie on the table, you think "Mom did some baking today," or "Brother went to the store," or anything but "A cookie monster from Valhalla granted me a snickerdoodle because I rubbed a magic lantern and prayed." "God did it" is the answer of a man too lazy to do science, or incapable of suspending judgment until the true cause of an event is tracked down.

Others say Christian miracles are real, but nothing special. Miracle-working gurus crowd the banks of the Ganges: Sai Baba, Mother Meera, the Bagwan Rajneesh. Empress Jadis puts on a show most every day. Gain *mana* or *qi*, and you, too, may speak a Deplorable Word, or at least mold elements into a ring and zap a nosy nephew off to another world.

Having heard from David Hume's disciples as a student at the University of Washington, I went to Asia at age twenty-two wondering if God were real. China had closed its temples and churches, and banned gods, aside from Money, Power, and "Mr. Science." India, Thailand, and Taiwan, by contrast, were choked with gurus, spirit houses, shamans cutting their backs in the street, ten-foot pantomime deities stalking back alleys at twilight, idols ported through slums by girls in safaris. I studied sects in which the supernatural seemed a daily event, and scientific ideologies in which only the course of Nature was accepted. I also witnessed things that seemed to undermine the "God hypothesis" in other ways: sexual slavery, religious riots, people who had been disfigured to elicit pity as beggars.

Nevertheless, I returned from Asia more confident of Christ.

For it seemed that the White Witch got one thing right. Aslan's magic was different. Contrary to Hume, Christian miracles do not "violate" Nature, slap her around, treat her rudely, or inconvenience her in any way. Neither are they "normal," "common," or "under our control." Miracles resemble Creation itself: effect follows cause, and creates beauty, which like woods, streams, mountains, and sky, glorify God. They do not turn humans into guinea pigs or stone: like Father Christmas, they offer gifts that fit our callings. Like the constructive processes of biology— eating, drinking, loving, birthing, healing — they enhance our humanity.

What are "miracles?" One must define a phenomenon to know whether it occurs. Keep your ring in your pocket this chapter: we'll jump between Narnia, Taiwan, First Century Palestine, and distant stars. (Change rings before you get too close to those hotties!) I will argue that miracles in the Christian sense do not "violate Nature," but fulfill her, and that is one way to know the real thing when we see it.

By David Hume's definition, only if natural laws are broken can one say a miracle has occurred. (Not counting the dreamy sense in which tulips blossoming in spring are a miracle.) So walking on water or rising from the dead pass. But when Jesus told Peter to go fishing to pay taxes, and he found a gold coin in the fish's mouth, that wasn't really a miracle because one can explain it naturally: fish swallow lures, why not coins?

Hume's definition carries two fatal flaws. First, "violation of the laws of Nature" isn't what the Bible means by the word. If skeptics hope to debunk Christian miracles, they must direct their arguments against the Christian concept of them. And second, Hume's definition demands a degree of knowledge that mortals cannot possess, especially in light of modern science.

Miracles as Signs

The most common word for miracle in the New Testament is *semeyon* (σημειον), or "sign," related to "semiotics." This term is used seventy-seven times. Another word used sixteen times is *teras* (τερας) a "wonder," or perhaps "sight," usually in the phrase, "signs and wonders."

"Stop!" "Merge!" "Road work ahead!" "El Paso, 220 miles!" Road signs point to a destination, or warn against a traffic hazard. The ancients believed that almost anything could be a sign from the gods, especially dreams and the flights of birds. A "sign" need not break the laws of physics, it need only let us know, "God is here." "Walk this path." "Rome will be victorious." "No crossing, train coming."

Aslan gives Jill four "signs by which I will guide you in your quest" to help Eustace and her find the lost prince of Narnia: none involves suspension of natural law. Aslan has told them to repeat the signs when they descend into the murky lowlands. First, greet an old friend. (They missed that one.) Second, look for the ruins of a giant city, and third: "You shall find a writing on a stone in that ruined city, and you must do whatever the writing tells you."

Puddleglum and the two children fight through a snowstorm to reach Harfang, the city of the Gentle Giants, before the doors close for the night. Eustace and Jill are thinking about warm baths, hot meals, and comfortable beds. The travelers wade through snow across a flat tableland above which rise strangely regular cliffs. They escape the storm by crawling through tunnels that shift directions at right angles.

Later, trapped in Harfang, the snow is washed away. The travelers gaze out a window and see ruins of a giant city below them, upon which the words "UNDER ME" are clearly visible. The tunnels they crawled through were part of one letter "E."

They escape Harfang, make their way far under the city (as instructed) across a dark sea to an underworld palace, where they meet an effete young dandy who informs them that in fact, no miracle took place: neither violation of Nature nor even message from God. What they read as a "sign" had a natural explanation:

> Those words mean nothing to your purpose… Those words are all that is left of a longer script, which in ancient times, as (the queen) remembers, expressed this verse:
>
> "Though under Earth and throneless now I be,
>
> Yet, while I lived, all Earth was under me."[1]

Jill and Eustace hear this naturalistic explanation of their "sign" and experience a crisis of faith: "This was like cold water down the back to Scrubb and Jill, for it seemed to them that the words had nothing to do with their quest at all, and that they had been taken in by a mere accident."

But Puddleglum again proves the sounder thinker. They had, after all, found the giant city, then been "lucky" enough to escape Harfang. And the children had flown on the breath of a lion! Under the circumstances, their doubts were as unreasonable as those of Doubting Thomas, after all the miracles he had seen. "Don't you mind him," said Puddleglum. "There are no accidents. Our guide is Aslan; and he was there when the giant king caused the letters to be cut, and he knew already all things that would come of them, including this."

---

[1] This recalls the famous poem by Percy Shelley, who like Lewis attended University College in Oxford, and whose talent he admired:

> "My name is Ozymandias, king of kings:
> Look on my works, ye Mighty, and despair!'
> Nothing beside remains. Round the *decay*
> Of that colossal wreck, boundless and bare
> The lone and level sands stretch far away."

Communication is contextual, in other words. A hand wave, a kiss, a smack, "I love you," "Take a hike," all mean or are signs of different things at different junctures in a drama.

Yale philosopher Nicholas Wolterstorff suggested that the Bible itself is like that message on the stones of the ruined city. The Bible, he argued, may sometimes be "appropriated discourse," language borrowed from one context that gives new meaning in another. C. S. Lewis agreed. In *Reflections on the Psalms*, Lewis said the Bible may involve "the taking up of a literature to be a vehicle of God's word." Early Christians saw that Jesus brought out new meaning from many layers of Jewish Scriptures. Puddleglum's insight helps us to see that whether or not the authors of Old Testament books had a clear vision of Jesus Christ in mind, what they wrote may still miraculously point to him.

God takes the initiative to speak. He can do so through any object: a donkey, the ruins of a giant king's boast, or even a cheeseburger at McDonald's.

Aslan in Asia

I was broke. I was trying to prod people into rescuing aboriginal girls who had been forced into prostitution. But a year in Youth With a Mission (YWAM), and the amazing stories I heard about God's provision, made me hope He would provide for my needs, too, without asking. This didn't always seem to work, and now I found myself out of cash, out of food aside from a little peanut butter, even out of soap and toilet paper. My parents had sent me a check, which seemed like an answer to prayer. But when I took it to the bank, they said, "Come back on Monday."

I spent some of my last coins to take a train to Taipei and buy a few munchies for breakfast. I walked to New Park a few blocks from the old station, and paced back and forth under a leaden sky. "Lord!

Why don't you provide for my needs! I'm here to do Your Will!" No reply. "I don't even have money to buy a hamburger!" Still nothing. "I love that song, 'Great is Thy Faithfulness,' but how can I sing it now?" I even tried threats. "If you won't provide for me, I'll go home! Who needs this?" (This felt as hollow as a threat to suicide.)

Tired of talking (it seemed) to an empty sky, I headed towards the north entrance of the park, where I noticed a pretty girl reading an English-language newspaper. I struck up a conversation in Chinese. She asked what I was doing in Taiwan, and I grudgingly explained I had come to tell people about God. As I stood up to leave, she asked my name.

"Ma Dewei (馬德偉)."

"Ma Dewei! You're Ma Dewei! Really?"

A few years before, this girl had lost her purse at National Taiwan University, several miles away. She went to Lost and Found, and there it was! She opened the purse and found her money, along with a note in crude Chinese: "God loves you. Ma Dewei.")

She remembered that name (and miracle of miracles, could read it!), then years later, "accidentally" ran into the American who had found her purse: myself.

To say "thanks," she took me to a nearby McDonald's for lunch. Part way into the meal, I remembered my complaint that I was too broke to buy a hamburger. (I had ordered a cheeseburger.)

That evening, two Chinese friends invited me home for dinner (the only time they had done so: I rarely had western food, and this was a delicious stew). I left early to speak to a small gathering near my apartment, and was unexpectedly given a little money. The woman leading the meeting suggested that we close by singing, "Great is Thy Faithfulness!" On Monday I arrived at the bank with a coin or so in my pocket, a full stomach, and a feeling of having been gently schooled.

Was that series of events a "miracle?" Not by Hume's definition. Meeting someone, and eating a meal at McDonalds, did not violate any laws of genetics, nutrition, or volcanology.

Yet like a sign, it pointed me in a certain direction, making that path more rational to follow.

The Problem of Measurement

All miracles can be explained away, if you wish. No measurements are exact, and our memories, senses, and friends are all fallible. Bolts of lightening must strike somewhere: why not on Elijah's altar, just after he prayed? Uncle Andrew can always hear just barking and braying from the talking animals, if he chooses.

Perhaps in a metro of 4.5 million people, running into that girl was just luck. Many events happen in a lifetime, and billions of people inhabit our world. Everyone "gets lucky" sometimes. (Even to be born!) Why is it strange that friends would welcome me to their home? Or that I would be given a gift to pay for speaking? Or perhaps I am making my hamburger story up! I can offer no physical proof that any of it occurred. (It did!)

The second problem with saying miracles must "violate the laws of Nature" is that genuine violations of natural law can never be proven, even in theory. Werner Heisenberg showed that you cannot measure both a subatomic particle's exact location and its velocity, no matter how good your instruments may be. Almost all we know comes through minds, senses, and people, each a bridge of frazzled vines across a chasm in Nepal. We can always find reasons, or excuses, to deny that some event is supernatural. (However improbable.)

The most famous miracle, after the Creation, is Jesus' resurrection from the dead. But in *The Case Against God*, philosopher Michael Martin offers many possible explanations for Easter. Paul hallucinated! The evangelists made the story up! Peter saw what he wanted to see. A quantum accident occurred. Some "unknown laws of nature" returned Jesus to life. The disciples met a Jesus look-alike! "Finite Miracle Workers" (FMW—Leprechauns? Elves?), reanimated their teacher!

Martin's suggestions were mostly pretty silly, just throwing mud against a wall to see if anything would stick. But these proposals remind us of the limits of certainty. Life is a gamble. Maybe your wife is a cyborg or hallucination, your marriage certificate a forgery, or Finite Mundane Workers downloaded an "I do" memory chip into your neurons. Philosophers point out, some with apparent conviction, that this whole universe may be a computer simulation.

When I ask an audience how many have experienced miracles, often a third or more raise their hands. This fits a Pew survey cited by Craig Keener, showing that thirty-four percent of Americans claim to have witnessed or experienced divine healing (*Miracles*, 204), and that Christians in Brazil, Chile, Guatemala, and Kenya are even more likely to make that claim (237). Ask these people to tell their stories (as both Keener and I have done), and many seem credible. Some confront one with Lucy-like choices: either this person is a remarkable liar, completely deluded (however sane she seems!), or materialism is toast.

But neither a natural nor a supernatural explanation can ever be completely ruled out. If you pray, and fire falls from heaven and consumes the bull, you might just have caught a lucky bolt. (Storms had been reported in the area when Elijah conducted this experiment.) Or you, and the prophets of Baal, may all be brains in a vat.

Faith, like reason, is an invitation. It is an open Wardrobe door, not a whip or a cattle prod. Fledge the flying horse told his human companions, "I've a sort of idea He likes to be asked." Miracles give one the impression He also likes to ask us.

But a serious skeptic should also be doubtful of his doubts. Having experienced such "coincidences," why should I (or Jill and Eustace) dismiss the more amazing series of events that Pauline Hamilton recounted as a missionary in Taiwan? Or my friend Don Richardson, who brought the Gospel to headhunters and cannibals in New Guinea? Or the providential earthquake that that shook the Chinese court in 1665 and saved the lives of two Jesuit missionaries and two Chinese Christians? St. Augustine records his experience of miracles in the late Roman world, and it was through purported miracles that Patrick escaped slavery, then returned to convert Ireland.

The Dai people in southern China are Theraveda Buddhists, aside from a few outcastes whom missionaries befriended. These rejects gathered in a little village on the outskirts of the regional capital. Under communist persecution, many forgot their Christian faith. A young Dai man in that village suffered severe back problems. Some suggested going to a Buddhist healer, but someone else said, "No, we're Christians." So they prayed for him and, they told me, he was healed. And so the village revived, and the young man drove me on his motorcycle to a church in the countryside, down bumpy roads that almost put my back out.

I stayed at the home of a shoe manufacturer and preacher in Zhejiang Province. He told me that he had once come down with throat cancer. He couldn't afford the medicine doctors said might prolong his life. Fellow Christians gathered to pray for him. He said he saw a vision of Jesus, who told him to preach the Gospel. He was instantly healed, he claimed, and took me to the top of a hill behind his house, where he pointed to villages where he and his fellows preached and healed. He did not want my money (though he asked for a book on Buddhism I had brought), and well understood the dangers of a preaching career in the hostile environment of communist China.

If you ask Christians in China how it is that under an often-murderous communist regime, and in the face of entrenched Chinese faiths, the Church has grown from two to some eighty million believers, you often hear stories like that. Miracles are also often cited by those who come to faith in Africa, India, and the Muslim World, as Keener and others show.

Maybe all those stories are lies. Maybe they are told by the gullible or delusional. But in my experience, such stories are often told late at night, in small apartments, perhaps over bowls of popcorn, by people who seem steady enough. And I know my experiences were real. On what grounds should I dismiss those that are a bit more remarkable, told in private by people who have nothing to gain?

But, you say, miracles occur in all religions. Which should we believe?

For one thing, the White Witch saw that "magic" comes in different forms.

Meeting a Magician

For my Masters of Arts degree at the University of Washington, I studied the True Buddha Movement, interviewing its founder, Lu Shengyan, and some of his followers. Lu's books were full of supernatural encounters with rival gurus and told of confrontations with dragons and the "god of Mount Rainier." (His head temple was a mile or two from Microsoft in the Seattle suburbs.) Most who talked with me claimed supernatural confirmation of Master Lu's powers, frequently in dreams, and often through healings.

A young woman who had come to the United States with her parents and brother to escape race riots in Indonesia told me the family's interest in True Buddha came about through her father's psychic abilities. "Sometimes my father had a dream, and the dream came true. Sometimes he like get the sixth sense, you know? Like there's something wrong or something going to happen, he always sense it." A doctor raised by an Aleut grandmother in Alaska who taught him the gods of the trees and other plants told me of a dream in which "Guru Lu held his hand out and light emitted over the crown (of my head)." A mechanic from Brunei with little education, though he spoke about seven languages, told me Lu was different because "He's become Buddha already." He believed Lu had saved his life in a car crash, and had accurately predicted the death of his father-in-law. The Cambodian mother of a child sleeping on the floor during a Saturday night service explained why she placed her faith in Living Buddha Lu: "I asked Master Lu about something that no one would know about my life— there was a certain secret that no one knew and I asked him and he knew." She claimed that, "The majority of the teaching is transmitted to my mind."

I first heard about the sect from two former friends of Lu, who left because of unsettling tantric rituals involving human substances, and their belief that the spirits visiting Lu were hostile.

Master Lu exposed his rivals as workers of "black magic" (a similar guru in the Bay Area), or fake living Buddhas (at the Tibetan temple in North Seattle where part of *Little Buddha* was filmed). He told wonderful stories, and his paintings were playful and fun. A follower invited me to his beautiful mansion against the Cascade Mountains. There Master Lu interrogated me, surrounded by disciples watching to see what would happen. They had told me to expect a sign when I met Lu. I saw an eagle fly overhead as we spoke, but it gave no sign. I began driving back over the dirt road away from his house, and saw an elk, but again, it gave no sign. Before I reached the pavement, though, a billboard appeared on my left: "Believe in the Lord Jesus Christ, and you and your family will be saved." That sign seemed more legible.

I have met other would-be founders of new religions, and studied the lives of more: Apollonius, Mohammed, Milarepa, Joseph Smith, Hong Xiuquan, Sai Baba, Jim Jones, Qing Hai. Many, including Master Lu, remind me of Queen Jadis or Uncle Andrew: people who use powers real or feigned to amass gold, bed mates, and command others by trickery. It seems that usually, the best gurus do the least magic: Confucius, Socrates, Lao Zi, Tolstoy, Gandhi, the present Dalai Lama, George Orwell, Jordan Peterson.

Like Trumpkin, I am often tempted to doubt. In years of wandering Asia, interviewing Living Buddhas and the like, and researching religion, I have never felt the slightest impulse to believe any wonder-working guru, besides "the Lord Jesus Christ." Dr. Kirke described some of the qualities that make the gospels unique, in the last chapter. But Aslan's magic was also of a different character, as the White Witch recognized.

Magic vs. Miracle

Eustace got to the nub of the matter in a chat with Jill about how to get to Narnia:

Jill: "You mean we might draw a circle on the ground—and write things in queer letters in it—and stand inside it—and recite charms and spells?"

Eustace: "Well...I've an idea that all those circles and things are rather rot. I don't think [Aslan would] like them. It would look as if we thought we could make him do things. But really, we can only ask him."

Eustace knew this because he had met Aslan on a previous visit to Narnia.

Narnian sailors and three English stowaways landed on a mountainous island after a rough voyage. An English boy named Eustace had cut himself from his shipmates during that voyage. He whined constantly, stole water, and played a cruel prank on Reepicheep the talking mouse. He liked animals if they were dead and pinned on paper: Reepicheep moved too much for his taste. The boy was a "little tick" himself. On the island, he wandered off to escape work, took a wrong turn in the fog, found himself in a remote valley, and watched a dragon die before his eyes. A torrential squall drove him into the dragon's cave, where he fell asleep thinking Uncle Andrew's thoughts after him, about riches, power, and revenge, while lying atop a dragon's hoard.

Notice the verb Lewis uses to describe Eustace's discovery upon waking: "He realized that he was a monster cut off from the whole human race." Not, he realized that he had *become* a dragon, but that he *was* one. Scales and talons revealed what his heart had long since grown into: "There was a boy called Eustace Clarence Scrubb, and he almost deserved it. I can't tell you how his friends spoke to him, for he had none."

Eustace had long cultivated his inner reptile by scorning others. As a teacher, I am tempted to blame his classmates for not bringing an isolated student into their circles. Aslan gives the little snob (a lot like Lewis himself as a lad) tougher love.

The boy had been a dragon all along. A dragon lacks "I-thou" relationships, seeing others as food, victims, or rivals. Eustace had been thinking with his lizard brain, maybe why he liked beetles. This transformation revealed what he already was.

At first Eustace thought of exploiting his serpent form to take revenge. But then the horror of his condition came over him.

The miracle Aslan did in restoring his outer form helps define how Christian miracles differ from magic. To borrow from another of Lewis' novels, how could Aslan meet Eustace face to face, until he had a face? Facing his true condition as a dragon was a precondition for becoming, or beginning to become, "a real boy." For that change would be a voyage itself:

"For some five days they ran before a south-south-east wind, out of sight of all lands and seeing neither fish nor gull. Then they had a day when it rained hard till the afternoon. Eustace lost two games of chess to Reepicheep and began to get like his old and disagreeable self again ...."

Read the long collections of letters from C. S. Lewis which Walter Hooper edited, and one notes a similar process. As a young skeptic, Jack was a self-confessed snob (undeniably brilliant) with a taste for sadomasochism. He begrudged his father for his own dependence, for his father's failure to visit when he was wounded in France, and for irritating eccentricities that, he admitted later, seemed lovable in other old men. In Lewis' letters, one can watch his life expand over the years, a growing kindness, and a steady prayer life that nurtured that growth.

Eustace likewise realized that true miracles are not tricks or mastery of formulae, but part of a life-enhancing relationship. This is not because they are unscientific, but because God is the One wearing the lab clothes, working on us, through experience.

The contrast between I-Thou miracles and I-It magic is clear from the beginning. Aslan sings animals into being, gives them reason, and teaches them to talk. God created man and woman in His image. Uncle Andrew treats children like guinea pigs, and guinea pigs like firecrackers. Queen Jadis uses the magic of her voice to commit genocide, and tries to scramble Aslan's brains. Magic (in this sense) makes people less human. Miracles point people to God, restoring, and developing, our humanity, as a part of the Song of Creation.

Mark Studdock, in *That Hideous Strength*, was faced with a superficially opposite, but equally diabolical temptation that would also sap his humanity. Frost, Wither, and Hardcastle were characters in whom inhumanity had set: souls frozen, faded, or fortified against their own best nature. But Mark's character was still in flux: "From now onwards till the moment of final decision should meet him, the different men in him appeared with startling rapidity and each seemed very complete while it lasted. Thus, skidding violently from one side to the other, his youth approached the moment at which he would begin to be a person."

Are miracles "arbitrary," as some call them? No. They glorify God, enhance our humanity and underline the integrity of creation.

Miracles Crown Nature

Scientists set their ears to the ground to hear the harmonies of Creation. Objects around us— lady bugs, blades of grass, redwood forests— follow patterns set by underlying forces. Beat itself emerges from Nature: the rhythm of hearts, seasons, ripples on water.

Even stars have tempo. A "classical" Cepheid variable is a massive young star with an atmosphere of ionized helium (missing one of its electrons). The closest such star is Polaris Aa, part of the North Star, some 400 light years away. As the star contracts, it heats, releasing radiation. The radiation knocks the second electron out of the helium, and the nucleus absorbs light, veiling the star. As the atmosphere heats up with absorbed radiation, it expands. Expansion makes it cool, like air rising over a mountain. The cooler helium then loses energy and bonds again with electrons. The star's atmosphere thus expands and contracts like a jellyfish, brightening and dimming over a week or month, like a heart four times bigger than our sun.

Song has melody as well as rhythm. Scientists who search for extraterrestrials (SETI) would eventually get bored watching a Cepheid variable. They want to hear notes that bespeak intelligence— intent, purpose, meaning within pattern.

Uncle Andrew, on the other hand, feared such signs. He heard the lion's songs as growls. He watched Nature unfold and saw only material processes. Queen Jadis knew that the lion was singing the world into being (the devil believes, and trembles.) But she did not understand the "deeper magic still."

Like Tom Bombadil, Aslan cared little for jewelry. "You don't need rings when you are with me," he told Digory and Polly, when they took the Aslan Express from Narnia back to London. He summoned Nellie in the other direction with a "long single note, not very loud but full of power." She came "not by any tiresome magic rings, but quickly, simply and sweetly as a bird flies to its nest." Indeed she was coming home, because true miracles make you more of what you were meant to be. They are not interruptions to the music of Nature, but its "finishing touches."

In the gospels, too, disciples are called by clear, simple notes of power. "Who is this man, that even the wind and waves obey him?" A man born blind is given sight. A twelve-year-old girl is raised from the dead, then fed. Tolkien mentioned this last detail in a letter to his son in 1944. He compared that girl to a boy who was healed in modern times, announced, "I'm hungry now," and ate cake, chocolate, and "enormous potted meat sandwiches." Tolkien concluded, "So plain and matter-of-fact: for so miracles are."

Creation shows integrity. True miracles do not make one bark like a dog, barf up stone sex organs as the Indian guru Sai Baba pretended to, or accumulate Rolls Royce like the Bagwan Rajneesh. The best magic does not "transgress the laws of nature." It harmonizes with the song of Creation on a higher key. Now Nellie will serve as Queen of Narnia, and her husband will dig in the earth and straighten out quarrels between talking animals.

God may work miracles outside the Christian tradition. Who am I to tell Him not to? And the Church holds plenty of faith healers who manipulate "even the elect," if possible. If church magic makes you less than human, distracts from the Creator's song, or encourages you to idolize unworthy objects, look for Uncle Andrew or the White Witch pulling strings behind the pulpit.

The line between Miracle and Magic is like that between Science and Pseudo-Science.

Lewis knew that astrology and astronomy, alchemy and chemistry, grew up as twins, like Romulus and Remus struggling to control Rome. Augustine recounted miracles that he and friends experienced, but coldly debunked astrology. The Church condemned the idea that the stars determine our fate. But tides show that heavenly bodies can affect the Earth. We now know that the gas giants Jupiter and Saturn shield Earth from comets, while other heavenly bodies help stabilize our planet's orbit. So it would be unfair to blame pious Medieval scientists like Johannes Kepler for thinking the planets influence us individually.

But both black magic (a pseudo-science) and vivisection (an inhumane science) abuse the innocent for power. Likewise, ancient kings sacrificed concubines, ministers, or slaves to serve them in the next world. This was the attitude of Jadis and Uncle Andrew.

Eustace, by contrast, prays, "Thy will be done."

Perhaps this view of miracles may help reconcile evolution and design. Just as God may use a weathered memorial to tell travelers which way to turn, so flowers and animals may emerge from the earth both by natural processes, and at Aslan's command.

Further Reading

Keener's long book *Miracles* should be read with care, since he argues both that reports of miracles are common, and that some seem credible. These two claims should be clearly distinguished. His more recent *Miracles Today* is an easier introduction to the same subject. Many books by missionaries mention miracles, including Don Richardson's *Peace Child* and *Lords of the Earth*, Pauline Hamilton's *To a Different Drum*, and broader surveys like Tony Lambert's *China's Christian Millions* and David Aikman's *Jesus in Beijing* (see my review in *Christianity Today*.) Augustine attacks astrology in Book V of *The City of God*.

David Hume's essay "On Miracles" is mentioned in this chapter, along with Michael's Martin's *The Case Against God*, and Tim McGrew's article on miracles in the *Stanford Encyclopedia of Philosophy*, which rebuts Hume. Also referred to is Nicholas Wolterstorff's *Divine Discourse: Philosophical Reflections on the Claim that God Speaks*, which takes a position much like Lewis stakes out in *Reflections on the Psalms*. Thomas Cahill tells the story of St. Patrick and what Irish conversion meant for Europe in *How the Irish Saved Civilization*. (St. Patrick's *Confessions* gives his story.) *The Life of Milarepa* and *The Life of Apollonius of Tyana* can, I believe, both be found online. Deborah Layton's inside account of People's Temple, *Seductive Poison*, may tell you more than you want to know about Jim Jones.

SEVEN

The Witch's Revenge

"Fool, did you think that by all this you would save the human traitor?
Now I will kill you instead of him as our pact was and so the Deep
Magic will be appeased. But when you are dead what will prevent me
from killing him as well? And who will take him out of my hand then?
Understand that you have given me Narnia forever, you have lost your
own life and you have not saved his. In that knowledge, despair and
die." The Lion, the Witch and the Wardrobe

So says the Empress Jadis to Aslan, backed by her merry band of
hags, ogres, wraiths, horrors, efreets, sprites, orknies, wooses, ettins,
and her lupine secret police, who together have mocked, beaten,
and shaved "the great cat." At an earlier interview, she asked him:

"Have you forgotten the Deep Magic?"

By "magic" she did not mean supernatural signs, but something
like karma: "You at least know the Magic which the Emperor put
into Narnia at the very beginning. You know that every traitor belongs to me as my lawful prey and that for every treachery I have
a right to a kill."

The moral law is "magic" because it is more than the physical
facts of Nature or even the biological laws of struggle for survival.
If you do justice, love mercy, and walk humbly with God, you transcend mere animality. Evolution itself, Dawkins admits, cannot

tell us how to live. Our awareness of good and evil is "magic" in the sense that it lies outside of physical or biological laws. We desire not merely daily bread, but justice.

The specific "lawful prey" Jadis referred to was Edmund, who had betrayed Narnia and his siblings. If such crimes were not paid for, the system would crash: "Unless I have blood as the Law says, all Narnia will be overturned and perish in fire and water."

Hero and villain agree on that, but Susan wonders if capital punishment for a first offense by a minor isn't excessive. "Oh, Aslan!…Can't we—I mean, you won't, will you? Can't we do something about the Deep Magic? Isn't there something you can work against it?"

Aslan frowns and asks, "Work against the Emperor's Magic?"

Yet there is a deeper magic: divine grace, love that sacrifices itself for another. So the lion-sage climbs the hill to the Stone Table. His is not a philosopher's death, like Socrates calmly drinking hemlock. His is a lover's death, and he is not stoical along the way:

"Are you ill, dear Aslan?"

"No. I am sad and lonely. Lay your hands on my mane so that I can feel you are there and let us walk like that."

Jesus, too, prayed in sorrow in the Garden of Gethsemane, and asked that the cup he was about to drink be taken from him. He then climbed Golgotha carrying a cross upon his lacerated back. Pascal read the story in astonishment, and asked who taught their authors "the qualities of a perfectly heroic soul:"

> Do they not know how to paint a resolute death? Yes, for the same Saint Luke paints the death of Saint Stephen as braver than that of Jesus Christ. They make him, therefore, capable of fear, before the necessity of dying has come and then altogether brave. But when they make Him so troubled, it is when He afflicts Himself; and when men afflict Him, He is altogether strong.

A mob of Social Injustice Warriors gathers to cancel Aslan. They, too, are more passionate than the city council that killed Socrates. They resemble the frenzied women in Euripides' play *Bacchantes*, or crowds that attack cops, Copts, Jews, Chinese, African Americans, or counter-revolutionaries. This is a lynching, not just an assassination. It is an assertion of group power, an act of "magic" by which Jadis means to rule Narnia forever.

Phillip Pullman found the scene maudlin and artificial. Lewis was "hijacking the emotions that are evoked by the story of the Crucifixion and Resurrection in order to boost the reader's concern about Aslan...."

Or perhaps the problem is the Christian story itself, and the very notion of redemptive sacrifice.

Atheist John Loftus wrote a book called *The Outsider Test for Faith: How to Know Which Religion is True*. I responded with *How Jesus Passes the Outsider Test: The Inside Story*. Following C. S. Lewis, I argued that one reason the Gospel spread was because "pagans" saw it as fulfilling their traditions. (See Chapter Ten.) London-based talk show host Justin Brierley invited us both onto his Unbelievable program to debate the matter. There I pointed out that the idea of God or the holy man sacrificing himself for humanity is "crucial" in ancient China and India. The crucifixion does not stand outside such traditions at all: it is a Master Key that fits many locks.

Loftus admitted that "lots of different cultures" affirmed the importance of sacrifice. But the whole notion, he scoffed, was just "primitive nonsense."

Far from "hijacking" the story of Jesus when he wrote the Chronicles of Narnia in his late middle age, the idea of redemptive sacrifice first touched Jack Lewis as a small boy. He was casually reading Longfellow's *Saga of King Olaf*, when his eyes lit upon the words:

I heard a voice that cried.
Baldur the beautiful
Is dead, is dead …

Lewis suddenly felt with "sickening intensity" a desire for something "cold, spacious, severe, pale, and remote." Later, he learned how, in Nordic mythology, Loki tricked Thor into killing Baldur, leading to the death of the gods and ultimately to the dawn of a new world.

Frodo and Sam take the ring into Mordor on a hopeless quest to save the Shire. Harry Potter trudges out of Hogwarts to confront "He who cannot be named" and sure death, to save his friends. Tom Hanks and his platoon set out across the battlefields of Normandy after Private Ryan. Gandhi fasts to near death to stop riots in Calcutta. Martin Luther King faces police dogs and water hoses. "Superstitious nonsense?" On the contrary, "Take up your cross and follow me!" is magic deeper than the White Witch's self-love, or even the justice that she tactically demands.

Lewis' mother died of cancer shortly after he read those heart-breaking, magical words about the death of Baldur. "All settled happiness" was lost for him. Sacrificial love is why we celebrate Mother's and Father's Days, and is the glory of military graves.

So I told John Loftus that his failure to understand the cross is one reason his version of Secular Humanism does not "pass the outsider test for faith."

Skeptics who "don't get it" should follow Professor Kirke's advice, and read Plato. Though his own master died peacefully, Plato predicted the lynching of Aslan.

Plato at the Stone Table

Aristotle argued that tragedy is driven not by personality (to "boost the reader's concern about Aslan," as Pullman put it) but by plot. Aristotle's teacher explained why Aslan had to die.

Plato's *Republic* relates a conversation between Socrates and Glaucon on the relationship between good and evil. Imagine a man who wholeheartedly seeks to do what is right. Slandered, he remains "steadfast in the hour of death." Suppose such a hero should confront an alter ego who cloaks himself in virtue, but is bad to the bone. What will happen if these particles of ethical matter and anti-matter clash? What Glaucon describes in reply is quite different from the famously calm death of his own teacher:

"He shall be scourged, tortured, bound, his eyes burnt out, and at last, after suffering every evil, shall be impaled or crucified."

Aslan was shaven and bled, in sight of jeering spectators who took his suffering as proof of victory. But the nakedness that shamed Christ on the cross more truly unmasked those who danced at its foot. Jesus swallowed the cup of shame of dying for villains: "Father, forgive them, for they know not what they do."

Did St. Mark "hijack the emotions" of his readers by "culturally appropriating" this Platonic ideal?

Last night I watched an old episode of Star Trek, "The Empath." The plot is about advanced aliens who were deciding whether to save a world of empaths from a supernova. The ranking officers on the U.S.S. Enterprise, Captain Kirk, Mr. Spock, and Dr. McCoy, beamed down to the planet. When it became evident that one of them would need to risk death and torture, each plotted to suffer in place of his friends. (As Hermione and Harry fought over the Horcrux.) The alien judges witnessed the virtues of the Enterprise officers, and noted: "Those are the qualities that make a civilization worthy to survive."

But the empath was the "variable" tested in that petri dish: would she give her life to save Doctor McCoy? Was her world worth saving?

So is the idea of redemptive sacrifice a primitive superstition? Or a truth we cannot escape, either in our daily lives, or in the far reaches of space, among advanced aliens centuries hence?

Deep Magic at the Dawn of Time

Ancient civilizations were usually ruled by people like Queen Jadis. Agamemnon sacrificed his daughter to the goddess Artemis before setting out to conquer Troy. The Aztecs sacrificed thousands at a time to encourage the gods to renew the world. Bodies have been found in mounds across the Mississippi River from St. Louis, in tombs in Sumer, bogs in England, and in ancient graves in the modern cities of Zhengzhou and Anyang, central China. Poor folks made due with a sheep, dog, or dove.

The ancients hoped that new life would come through death. If someone else took their seat on the ferry across the River Styx, so much the better. A similar mindset may explain some cruelty in modern families, argued psychologist M. Scott Peck. Jane Eyre and Harry Potter served such a "scapegoat" function when young.

General Patton offered a famous distinction:

"No dumb bastard ever won a war by going out and dying for his country. He won it by making some other dumb bastard die for his country."

To sacrifice others is, indeed, generally preferred. But to sacrifice oneself for others is the deeper magic. As a young man, Lewis was moved by the myth of the god who died to make grain grow. James Frazer argued that religion evolved from this myth. Lewis' beloved tutor, William Kirkpatrick, was deeply influenced by *The Golden Bough*, as was Lewis himself, for a while.

The Christian story rubbed Lewis wrong, though, as it rubs Loftus wrong. In 1931, Lewis told his childhood friend, Arthur Greeves, that what held him back from faith in Christ was the doctrine of Redemption: "What I couldn't see was how the life and death of Someone Else (whoever he was) 2000 years ago could help us here and now—except in so far as his example helped us."

Like Loftus, Lewis found talk of Jesus' "sacrifice" or "the blood of the Lamb" either "silly" or "shocking." Yet unlike Loftus, he had come to believe that Truth must not merely negate the insights of other traditions:

"The question was no longer to find the one simply true religion among a thousand religions simply false. It was rather, 'Where has religion reached its true maturity? Where, if anywhere, have the hints of all Paganism been fulfilled?'"

"Rum thing, about the Dying God," his colleague Weldon told Lewis. "Seems to have really happened once." Then Hugo Dyson and J. R. R. Tolkien dropped in. Together, the trio strolled under chestnut trees along Addison's Walk in Magdalen College.

> What Dyson and Tolkien showed me was this: that if I met the idea of sacrifice in a Pagan story I didn't mind it at all: again, that if I met the idea of a god sacrificing himself to himself I liked it very much and was mysteriously moved by it: again, that the idea of the dying and reviving god (Balder, Adonis, Bacchus) similarly moved me provided I met it anywhere except in the gospels. The reason was that in Pagan stories I was prepared to feel the myth as profound and suggestive of meanings beyond my grasp even though I could not say in cold prose what it meant.

Tolkien, Lewis, and others had been reading *The Poetic Edda* in Icelandic, in which Baldur's father also gave himself up in death: "Nine nights I hung upon the Tree, wounded with the spear as an offering to Odin, myself sacrificed to myself."

The story of Christ, then, looked like a "true myth." It worked on one the same way these other stories did, except that "it really happened."

Lewis was a famous bookworm. When he first heard a bullet whiz past in France, he thought, "This is war. This is what Homer wrote about!" But on the Western Front, he must have recognized that sacrifice was not limited to literature. Sergeant Ayres was a "father-like" figure who apparently died of the same artillery round that wounded Lewis.

So Pullman could not be more wrong. Aslan didn't die to win artificial sympathy. The lion's act of love lay at the heart of Lewis' understanding of life. Great myths helped Lewis recognize in the Gospel, a key to a mystery with which Plato had grappled and Lewis would ponder in grownup fantasy as well as life: the "crossing" between Good and Evil.

Straight Meets Crooked

That Hideous Strength is an adult story about "lions" and "witches." In it, Mark Studdock, a young sociologist, has recently joined the National Institute for Coordinated Experiments (NICE). He is arrested for a murder he did not commit. His bosses use the bogus charge to mold Mark into a witch, essentially: one who exploits power to overthrow laws divine and English, and make Britain "always winter and never Christmas." Dr. Frost, a not-at-all-nice NICE official, tutors Mark in the local Cancel Culture. But his tutorial hits a snag. Mark comes to perceive a standard of the natural and healthy that opposes the NICE regime's twisted ways:

> It was all mixed up with Jane and fried eggs and soap and sunlight and the rooks cawing at Cure Hardy and the thought that, somewhere outside, daylight was going on at that moment... 'All that,' as he called it, was what he chose. If the scientific point of view led away from 'all that,' then be damned to the scientific point of view.

Narnia and the Shire are homelands of "all that," drawn from images of rural Oxford, Worcester, and Cornwall, where some

Inklings went on walking tours. Those imaginary worlds borrow English trees, flowers, mushrooms frying with eggs in a skillet, and beer and laughter at some local Prancing Pony late into the night.

But Studdock is confronted with the same problem Socrates introduced. Evil sits on the throne. Crooked meets Straight with an armed mob and a Jadis-like taste for public humiliation.

As part of his training in "objectivity," that is, in dragon-like detachment from humanity, Frost tells Studdock to trample on a crucifix. The young man suddenly sees what Glaucon had perceived 2500 years before:

> Most emphatically (the crucifix) did not belong to that idea of the Straight or Normal or Wholesome which had, for the last few days, been his support against what he now knew of the innermost circle at Belbury...His simple antithesis of the Normal and the Diseased had obviously failed to take something into account...
>
> Christianity was nonsense, but one did not doubt that the man had lived and had been executed thus by the Belbury of those days. And that, as he suddenly saw, explained why this image, though not itself an image of the Straight or Normal, was yet in opposition to crooked Belbury. It was a picture of what happened when the Straight met the Crooked, a picture of what the Crooked did to the Straight - what it would do to him if he remained straight. It was, in a more emphatic sense than he had yet understood, a *cross*.

The gospels shock us not merely because in them, we meet a good man, as startling as their portrait of Jesus is, still less for their common rabble of cowards and villains. We are shocked by the revolutionary *crossing* of good and evil. "Human culture is predisposed to the permanent concealment of its origins in collective violence," wrote Rene Girard. Official histories of Narnia under Queen Jadis would not have recorded the murder of Aslan, or would have accused him of horrible crimes to justify it. But the gospels, Girard noted, would have none of such political spin-meistering: rather than covering up and making excuses for Power, they rub our noses in the stench of corporate guilt.

A Witch on the Couch

M. Scott Peck returned to Christ after decades of seeking to help psychology patients. The puzzle for Peck, too, was the "cross" between good and evil. What does one do with the "demonic," the sheer nastiness of so many people? The "weirdness" of Jesus seemed to hold answers for the neurotic complexities of his patients.

Most people try to deny evil, Peck said. In ancient Hinduism and Buddhism, the New Age, and some forms of psychotherapy, evil is seen as an illusion, or something to be cured by science and progress. "The three monkeys—see no evil, hear no evil, speak no evil—are exalted to guruhood." Peck was a disciple of those sensory-deprived chimps for years, and wisely continued to stress the value of medicines, social programs, and affirmation, and the danger of unwittingly becoming the evil which we attack.

But Peck had met too many White Witches, and concluded that the reality of evil could not be denied.

Others give in and embrace the "dog eat dog" nature of life, he noted. Let Jadis, Miraz, Sauron, Voldemort, the Joker, and Thanos all jump into a hot tub for schnapps. Tom Flint is no more a villain than you or I, just more honest. We evolved to seek health, food, power and to "get lucky" at the expense of others. Mark Studdock fantasized about the "normal" act of eating eggs: but would not a chicken find that perspective cruelly species-centric? Even Jordan Peterson admits that "we all need a glimpse of the evil queen."

Peck found both optimism and pessimism partly true, but incomplete.

Like Studdock, Peck was shocked by self-sacrificial virtue. The intersection of good and evil on the cross converted Peck to what he called "a most unreasonable theology."

While it, too, acknowledges the reality of both good and evil, it does not consider them coequal. Not only does it hold the God of Light to be more powerful than Satan, the Prince of Darkness, it makes the outrageous claim that human evil has been defeated.

Which brings us back to the Stone Table.

What did Peck mean by calling Christianity "unreasonable?" He meant not only that good and evil intersect in the death of Jesus, but that Jesus embodied virtues that went beyond the "wise and the sensible." (As he described Moses, Buddha, Lao Zi, and Mohammed.) "Jesus, too, was wise, but he was also weird. I do not know how to describe him in purely human terms."

Peck had studied the human psyche all his life, and humility was not his most outstanding virtue. (The back cover of the book in which these comments appear describe his *The Road Less Traveled* as "arguably the most influential book of modern times.") So for Peck to admit his inability to explain Jesus was an "embarrassing" concession.

Portions of the gospels, Peck argued, echoing others cited by Professor Kirke in the last chapter, "reek of authenticity": "No one could have made up the man described in them. Something very unreasonable happened in the area of Palestine almost two thousand years ago—so unreasonable as to compel me to suspect that God really did 'come down to live and die as one of us.'"

After a life of studying religious violence and scapegoating, Rene Girard concluded that Jesus got the better of the mobs that crucified him, and of society which supports mob violence.

Pullman and Loftus miss such depths. Their failure to notice what is going on at the Stone Table shows how much Secular Humanists still have to learn from Christ.

Lewis took Jesus' oft-repeated words to his disciples, "Take up your cross, and follow me," seriously. He believed that while Jesus had died for the sins of all men, we must follow Christ through pain, for the good of our souls, and to help others. When his wife Joy was suffering from bone cancer, as she gained strength in her bones, Lewis welcomed his own painful bouts of osteoporosis, thinking perhaps God was allowing him to take on some of her suffering.

On August 9th, 1945, a B-29 called Bockscar dropped an atomic bomb above Urakami Valley north of Nagasaki, Japan. In sad irony, in that valley lived (and lives) much of the city's Catholic community, which had been persecuted for hundreds of years. (In 1597, twenty-six crosses were raised on a hill above where the city's train station now lies, with Christians upon them.) A doctor who treated the wounded after the war, Takashi Nagai, wrote a book called *The Bells of Nagasaki*, in which he argued that the Catholic community was suffering for Japan as a whole.

About the time those prophetic crosses were raised in Nagasaki, an obscure Chinese Catholic named Liu Ning looked at the Chinese character ten (十), or cross, and asked, "Isn't that what the Holy Law proclaims? The four corners show that our Lord died for all men in the world." The horizontal lines extend as if to embrace mankind. The vertical lines bisect heaven and earth. The cross of Christ likewise reaches across cultures to embrace truth in the suffering of a mother giving birth, of Socrates for his city, of soldiers (even Dumbledore's Army) for their comrades. Not only in Baldur, but Prajapati in India, the Suffering Servant in Israel, and the Sage in China, divinity dies to save. The White Witch missed this deeper magic.

But according to Aslan, there is a deeper magic still, beneath both creation and sacrifice—the miracle of re-creation.

Plato foresaw no sequel to the good man's death. But the Viking poet believed Baldur the Beautiful would come back to life after the realm of the gods was destroyed. An ancient Jewish prophet also seemed to catch a whiff of the deepest magic of all:

Yet it was the Lord's will to crush him and cause him to suffer,
and though the Lord makes his life an offering for sin,
he will see his offspring and prolong his days,
and the will of the Lord will prosper in his hand.
After he has suffered,
he will see the light of life and be satisfied;
by his knowledge my righteous servant will justify many,
and he will bear their iniquities.

Further Reading

Beginning: Seek the meaning of the cross in the lives of those you love, and in fiction and heroic biography.

Advanced: Lewis tells his story in *Surprised by Joy*. The final letter in Volume I of Lewis' collected letters preserves his state of mind at the time. *The Scapegoat* gives a good summary of Rene Girard's arguments. A shorter summary can be found in Girard's article in *First Things*, April 1996: "Are the Gospels Mythical?" In my view, Girard offers an important perspective, but tries to explain too much by it. M. Scott Peck gives his view of Jesus in *In Search of Stones*: see also *People of the Lie*. Other books cited are mentioned in the chapter; I also refer to Jordan Peterson's article in Quillette, "For Our Own Good, We All Need a Glimpse of the Evil Queen." I borrow Jaroslav Pelikan's perhaps slightly free translation of Glaucon's words from his classic, *Jesus Through the Centuries*.

EIGHT

Deeper Magic from before the Dawn of Time

"Aren't you dead then, dear Aslan?"

"Not now!"

"But what does it all mean?"

"It means that though the Witch knew the Deep Magic, there is a magic deeper still which she did not know. Her knowledge goes back only to the dawn of time. But if she could have looked a little further back, into the stillness and the darkness before Time dawned, she would have read there a different incantation. She would have known that when a willing victim who had committed no treachery was killed in a traitor's stead, the Table would crack and Death itself would start working backwards..." The Lion, the Witch and the Wardrobe

Is the alleged resurrection of Jesus from the dead "cheating," to use Pullman's term, breaking the rules of the universe? Should we view Easter as an "extraordinary claim" that no amount of evidence should make us believe? Is there much evidence?

Suppose Aslan let Susan and Lucy, like the women in the gospels, run and tell their brothers the good news. "He is risen!" Should Peter and Edmund have believed them?

"Well, Lu, you were right about a world in the wardrobe. Sorry we didn't buy that one. But isn't this a bridge too far? I mean, Mr. Beaver's fish didn't come back to life! Maybe you're a little young to realize this yet, but sorry, animals die, and that's it. Yes, I'm afraid that includes talking animals. And yes, it means us, too."

Miracles are as easy to rationalize as sin. Suppose Ed were pouring over maps for the upcoming battle. Suppose he had also been reading David Hume at "that school of his," and watching Al Gore movies. He might find another explanation for Narnia's sudden warming trend: "This 'witch's winter' was actually caused by oscillating currents off the Lone Islands. With increased use of fossil fuels in the densely-populated cities of Calormen, Global Warming—if Narnia is a globe—was bound to kick in."

Wait by the graveyard, or butcher's, so long as you like. Surely Hume was right to say "uniform experience" opposes the notion that the dead can come to life again?

Ancient peoples knew death intimately. I mentioned how Agamemnon sacrificed his daughter before sailing to conquer Troy. This set off a ghastly family feud leading ultimately to the trial of Agamemnon's son Orestes for the murder of his mother. A play by Aeschylus describes how that trial was conducted on Mars Hill in Athens. The judge was the goddess Athena herself. The young man's defense lawyer, none other than the god Apollo, warned, "The blood of mortals seeps back into the Earth, the dead are not raised." So his client should not be executed.

Yet in that same forum, centuries later, St. Paul boldly announced to the city's elite that God had prepared a man to judge the world, calling all men to repent, and giving proof "by raising him from the dead." Paul later wrote to Christians in Corinth, sixty miles to the west: "If Christ has not been raised, your faith is in vain."

Easter remains the heart of the Christian message. What happened that morning? Time has not settled the debate. Christian scholars like Gary Habermas, Mike Licona, Timothy McGrew, and N. T. Wright have written thousands of pages arguing that Christ really did rise. At least fourteen eminent unbelievers have publicly debated William Lane Craig, asserting that he did not. Skeptics like Michael Martin and John Crossan have offered a host of natural explanations for the Easter Enigma, some of which I mentioned earlier.

What can a scene from a children's fantasy possibly add to all that scholarly thunder?

I argued that miracles represent a "deeper magic" that complements, and does not conflict with, the Song of Creation. I also pointed out that there is evidence that they sometimes occur. Professor Kirke briefly listed numerous historical reasons to believe the gospels.

Aslan offers three more lessons to help us figure out what happened Easter morning, having to do with Entropy, Creation, and Prior Probability.

Entropy and Creation

"Things fall apart." Grass withers. Flowers fade. Eyes weaken. Minds fog. And the whole universe, say physicists, is marching like an assembly of the damned to an inevitable "heat death" in which even particles of matter will break down into cosmic porridge, too cold for Mama Bear (or the constellation Ursa Major) to stomach.

Entropy is also known as "The Second Law of Thermodynamics" or "Murphy's Law." It describes the doom that faces not only our bodies and minds, but the world and every molecule in it. C. S. Lewis knew that fate as the "Twilight of the Gods," Ragnarok, from the epics he read with J. R. R. Tolkien and friends. In a recent comic version, Thanos (short for the Greek *thanatos*, or death) falls in love with Mistress Death and attains six "infinity stones" to kill half of all living beings as a love offering. Even the organization of quarks into atoms, atoms into molecules, molecules into organs, and organs into elephants, ravens, and flying horses, can be seen as local, rear-guard actions against relentless Fate.

Robert Frost warned that winter comes to relationships, too:

Some say the world will end in fire,
　Some say in ice.
From what I've tasted of desire
I hold with those who favor fire.
But if it had to perish twice,
I think I know enough of hate
To say that for destruction ice
Is also great
And would suffice.

No wonder Susan and Lucy wept. No wonder women came to anoint Jesus' tomb with incense, to disguise the smell of decay.

But rot raises a question both scientific and religious. What wound the universe up? A thing cannot decay that did not begin in a state of greater order. Clocks break: sand is merely scattered. In scientific terms, the universe must have begun in a "state of low entropy" for things to fall apart afterwards. The tendency for things to grow disordered defines life, including in the petri dish of Narnia. But that implies that we must look to the origin and purpose of a world to understand it, the "deeper magic" which called it into being.

Easter goes "deeper" than Entropy because before Creation, the universe must have been sung into a state capable of running down. Roger Penrose calculates the odds against the early universe appearing in its initial state of low entropy by chance at one in ten to the tenth to the 123rd power: a figure that would take all the fundamental particles in trillions upon trillions of universes our size just to write out. Physics itself demands some "deeper magic."

Aslan, the singer, admitted to the White Witch that the death of traitors (sin being one form entropy takes in the soul) was ordained at the start of the world. But the witch did not know the magic from before Aslan's Creation song.

The "deepest magic" is that death, too, will die. The fact that the universe began in a state of order, shows that the cracking of the stone, then "death working backwards," does not contradict ultimate laws. The witch saw the matchless power of Entropy within the system, but Aslan looked before the Big Bang (or "Big Song"). So the Resurrection was not "cheating." Aslan's story is simply less provincial than our common experience: evidence that Creation, or later local creation events like the first life, were not unique, because the universe is not entirely a closed system.

Perhaps all local acts of providence are signs of that bigger story, as a composer may drop in chords that echo the opening sonata of a symphony, unifying the piece. Discords warn the listeners that the composer has more to say than simple symmetries and harmonies can express. They are voices of life from outside the sterile pattern.

Did Frodo Cheat?

Was J. R. R. Tolkien "cheating" when he allowed Frodo's mission to succeed? Frodo did not, in the end, find strength to throw the Ring of Power into the lava under Mount Doom. But while quieter than Aslan's roar, Ultimate Power was also at work in Middle Earth. "You were meant to have the ring, Frodo. And that is some comfort," said Gandalf, wielder of the "Secret Fire," which refers to the Holy Spirit. Behind the scheming of Sauron and his minions, the betrayal of Saruman, the benevolent neglect of Bombadil, the shrewd suspicions of Farmer Maggot, or the scatter-brained kindness of Barliman Butterbur, the Hand of Providence (I am tempted to say, the Tao) was secretly moving.

Frodo is not quite a Christ figure. He is a hero who redeems by willing sacrifice. But like Ransom in Lewis' *Space Trilogy*, his power is mortal. Give Gandalf the ring, and he might be able to overthrow Sauron, but (Tolkien explained in a letter) its power would have conquered the proud wizard and twisted him into something evil.

By obeying the law of Spiritual Entropy and grabbing for power, Gollum set himself up for a fall. But God knows kung fu, and uses the strength even of enemies like Thanos, to defeat them.

Two Keys to the Past

You see a sign in front of a bank: "20 degrees." Who set it up? Who manufactured and maintains it? You don't know. But fat flakes of snow are settling onto it. So you say, "Of course! Water freezes at 32° so it is snowing, not raining."

Only you are in Japan, where temperatures are measured in Celsius, not Fahrenheit. 20° C would be 68° F, too warm for snow. Yet it is January, and cold, white flakes are piling up on your jacket. Perhaps the bank manager is eccentric, and studied in America. But bankers aren't known for whimsy. Maybe the gauge is broken. Or is that a dot? Maybe the temperature is 2.0° C, not 20°. It can snow a couple degrees above freezing.

Signs, then, must be read in context. How you interpret one depends on broader facts: Japanese measurements, the freezing temperature of water, corporate culture, the fragility of machines, perhaps some fog on your glasses.

The past explains itself to us in the same two ways: by evidence and by background knowledge. Our senses detect motion, scent, sound, flavor, and texture. We exploit media—airwaves, ink on paper, pixels on screen—to report events. Then we interpret the evidence furnished by minds, senses, and other people against all else that we think we know. We sift every claim through the filter called "prior probability:" a meteor's fall, a presidential election, Lucy's excited shouts that the Stone Table has cracked.

Did Jesus rise? The Christian scholar should win that debate easily enough, so long as she focuses on the first element, the historical evidence itself.

Evidence for the Resurrection

As we saw, even non-Christian scholars recognize N. T. Wright for his care, breadth of knowledge, and sophistication as an historian. In *Resurrection of the Son of God*, Wright concluded, after 700 pages of careful argument, "The proposal that Jesus was bodily raised from the dead possesses unrivaled power to explain the historical data at the heart of early Christianity."

As Wright showed, each gospel tells a slightly different version of the story, that resists attempts to read as mere "spin." Yes, Jesus did die: the Romans knew how to kill a man. No, a beaten, stabbed, whipped victim of a botched crucifixion never sallied forth half-starved from a tomb to convince his followers he was the Lord of Life. All attempts to find a parallel— Romulus, Inanna, Apollonius, Aslan—only underline the unique strength of evidence for the Easter story.

So why, then, did Susan and Lucy hardly believe their eyes? Why does Luke say that the apostles thought reports of the resurrection were "nonsense," and even when they saw Jesus, at first took him for a spirit? Matthew admits that "some doubted!" And John records Trumpkin's, I mean Thomas', demand: "Unless I see the nail marks in his hands and put my finger where the nails were, and thrust my hand into his side, I will not believe."

I understand. Like Mr. and Mrs. Beaver, First Century Jews thought that "Things would be made right when Aslan comes in sight": the Messiah would defeat the Roman legions, reign as king, and no doubt dispense liberal patronage. Every snow bank would melt, every flower would blossom.

Then it all came crashing down. Crowds turned against the man who had healed and fed them. "Crucify him!" came shouts from every direction. And Jesus put up no fight at all. He was beaten and mocked, and openly admitted that God had abandoned him. Panic spread through his little band of fishermen and tax collectors, their one pitiful sword tripping up the now-disgraced blowhard, "Peter the Rock."

Life had grabbed the wrong script. The Son of God was crucified like a thieving slave, shamed naked before the nation, hope draining under the whip along with his bodily fluids. Rome knew all about Shock and Awe, and torture was its natural sport.

Now you say he's risen? In secret? The disciples must have felt drained.

Yet Wright finds no "spectrum" of opinion about what happened among the earliest followers. All hopes suddenly focused in one direction. Every sermon in Acts, almost every letter of Paul, harps on one historical claim, agreed upon by hundreds of disciples, most of whom Paul said were still alive. "Jesus is risen!"

Oddly, the rumor began among women. The ancient Jewish historian Josephus warned against accepting evidence from women, "because of the levity and temerity of their sex." "Nobody inventing stories after twenty years, let alone thirty or forty, would have done it like that," Wright notes.

The first reports of the Resurrection diverged on superficial details, but agreed on the main facts. They bear "the puzzled air of someone saying, 'I didn't understand it at the time, and I'm not sure I do now, but this is more or less how it was.'" Even Philip Pullman admitted:

The confused, contradictory, almost breathless accounts of what happened after the sabbath when one woman, or two, or three, came to the empty tomb are vastly superior as storytelling —intensely realistic accounts of the confusions and contradictions on a morning when the grave was found to be empty, of a kind recognizable to anyone who's served on a jury and heard conflicting statements from witnesses.

Wright shows that the Resurrection stories also fit the pattern he calls "double similarity, double dissimilarity." They are Jewish, but no Jew ever invented their like. They lay the foundation of the Church to this day, but carry few of the interpretive elements common even in the gospels, still less "smooth" later Christian tradition.

Easter is "Jewish" because Hebrews believed in Creation and the goodness of matter, and the eventual conquest of death. "The resurrection matters for John because he is, at his very heart, a theologian of creation," Wright notes, which is why John echoes Genesis: "In the beginning was the Word." But Mr. and Mrs. Beaver dreamed of no such consummation of Narnia's story, nor did the Jews expect their Messiah to be lynched, then rise again. Easter is the historical "Big Bang" from which the Church shot out in all directions. But it only happened once. When Jesus appeared, "Some doubted," Matthew says, even among Jesus' closest disciples! Who? How many? How were their doubts resolved? Nothing is done with this embarrassing confession. Who would invent such a superficially damning detail?

Thoughtful historians have shown that there is a great deal of evidence for the resurrection. These are just a few examples: for many more, read the books mentioned at the end of the chapter, or listen to some of Craig's debates online. My friend Gary Habermas is presently writing an even more comprehensive work giving historical evidence for this central event in history. David Hume would ask, though: can there possibly be enough evidence?

How Much Evidence Do We Need?

"Extraordinary claims demand extraordinary evidence," we are told. Hume argued that we should prefer any explanation over a miracle. So might a one-celled organism born in a petri dish outside of office hours deduce that scientists do not exist, or never meddle with their potions.

Richard Lenski of Michigan State University has been tracking twelve E. coli populations, like twelve disciples, as they pass on the Gospel of their genomes for thirty-three years. (Over 73,500 generations, equivalent to more than a million years of human evolution.) Every day, small samples are frozen to provide snapshots of that day's progress. In one population, the bugs developed a taste for citric acid, or lemon flavoring, which is included in the flask medium.

Imagine what an E. coli philosopher in another flask would say of that "extraordinary claim." "Not likely! We live in a closed system. For the past 400 generations, no 'scientist' has put anything into or taken anything out of our flask. For 31,000 generations, and in eleven out of twelve populations of billions, no 'mutation' has taken place to render that lemony stuff edible. Our universal experience is that anything is more likely than such superstitious rumors."

But the point of the experiment is to look for unexpected developments.

Underworld gnomes only knew Narnia as a rumor. Rilian had never been to Bism. You can only know miracles do not happen if you know you live in a closed universe, just as you can know blue jays did not steal cookies off your plate if the sliding door is shut. But unless you see the whole world from before creation, before time and space were spun up, and know all the plans of its Creator, you cannot be sure your world is truly closed. Meaningful events are often rare: how many climaxes can a story experience?

That cymbals are seldom struck, does not prove there are no such instruments in the orchestra.

With imperfect brains and fallible senses, we rely on friends, teachers, and media that often err ("nothing but lies, libel, poppycock, propaganda, and pornography," Lewis once grumpily but poetically described newspapers. Imagine what he would say about Twitter!) Yet against all odds, we live in a universe that allows our hearts to beat. And when Susan blows her trumpet, sometimes help seems to come in remarkable ways. These may be clues to the meaning of our story. They should help us calculate what degree of skepticism to bring when Sue and Lu run down the hill and say, "Aslan is alive again!"

The name for such a calculation is "prior probability:" the factors we consider when determining how to understand that gauge outside the bank.

Prior Probability

Suppose I say, "I just flipped an unweighted coin twenty times, and got all heads!" Should you believe me? Ask two questions: (a) How likely is this result by chance? (About one in a million.) (b) How likely are the available explanations? (Such as lie, lunacy, or luck?)

If I say I flipped three heads in a row, you would shrug. If I said I'd done it 300 times in a row, you would doubt my coin or conscience. You'd "smell a rat."

Paul told the Committee for Skeptical Inquiry that met on Mars Hill, "God has given proof to everyone by raising (Jesus) from the dead." Like Apollo before them, most began to scoff. But Paul did not claim Easter was just a lucky event, like Charlie happening to find a coin and snagging the winning ticket to Willy Wonka's chocolate factory. His claim was that God acted for purposes central to the human story.

The prior probability of that act depends on answers to three questions: (1) Does God exist? (2) How likely is it that while allowing most bodies to decompose, He would raise one person dramatically from the dead? (3) What are the odds that that person would be Jesus?

(1) Most people believe in God. If the reasons I have given so far, such as creation, conscience, miracles, and the credibility of the gospels, seem insufficient, ask your believing friends why they believe. I especially recommend asking former missionaries, if you know any. Listen with an open heart and a critical mind.

(2) If God exists, would He raise someone from the dead? There are several reasons to think He might:

God is, by hypothesis, good, and should wish to give us hope.

The slings and arrows of cosmic fortune favored our planet, and life that arose on it, in mind-numbing ways. The very bacteria on our teeth reveal unfathomable complexity and the appearance of design. We feel, Lewis said, a desire for something that nothing in this world can satisfy. The appearance of sages like Socrates, Confucius, and Isaiah, and miracles in the lives of many great reformers, can be read as further "signs" denoting purpose in history.

To count, all you need is a brain, and maybe fingers. (Plus eyes or ears.) To study rocks, you need mind, vision, and touch. To study herbs, a nose and taste buds come in handy. If you wish to learn about wild Mongolian wolves, an element of mutuality appears: if the dog doesn't trust you, it may bolt, or attack. If you wish to know a human being, the initiative is even more equally shared, depending on relative intelligence, position, and power.

God's will cannot be calculated like a simple math problem. Neither can we isolate God and study Him like a glacier or a herd of musk oxen. God must take the initiative in our relationship, or we can never know Him. But there seem to be signs that God favors resurrections: counter-entropic creation; the rebirth of Nature in spring; prophecies that point to Easter; the centrality of the pattern Tolkien calls eucatastrophe in great fiction: our love for the "good disaster" may, if we are made in God's image, reflect His ultimate promised intent.

(3) If God wished to publicly rattle the chain of Thanatos and affirm someone's message by raising him or her from the dead, whom would He choose? Suppose God also wanted to reprimand oppressors. Martin Luther King might seem a good choice. His resurrection would not only signal hope, but tell us that God stands with the oppressed.

King's resurrection might send mixed messages about how to treat women, though, or force God to "pick sides" in American politics. Other Nobel Peace Prize winners, or say Confucius or Socrates, might do as well. If God wanted to "send a sign" by resurrection, the chance He would pick a victim of Auschwitz also seems higher than some random electrician or Senate lobbyist.

The words "UNDER ME" gain new meaning by placement within a significant story—the rescue of a lost prince and the salvation of Narnia. In the same way, Aslan's resurrection is a watershed in Narnian history: "When a willing victim who had committed no treachery was killed in a traitor's stead, the Table would crack and Death itself would start working backwards."

The lion's death would not just help one boy cheat fate, but make death begin "working backwards." This would be a step across a continental divide in history. Wright describes the Resurrection as a culmination of Israel's long tale of salvation.

So even aside from Christian theology, Jesus was far and away the most likely person in history to be raised for at least six reasons:

(1) Miracles do seem to happen sometimes, especially when he was around. One can take that as a "sign" that God was with him.

(2) The Jewish prophets pointed to Jesus. As Pascal saw, some clues were vague, others fairly clear. Joy Davidman, the Jewish poet who married C. S. Lewis, saw Christianity not as the religion of the *goyim*, but as the most vital modern form of Judaism.

(3) Lin Yutang, the great Chinese philosopher and man of letters, who compiled an anthology of Chinese and Indian literature, said that "no man has taught as Jesus taught." Scott Peck concurred, as did the Father of the Bengal Renaissance, Ram Mohan Roy, who published a booklet in 1820 entitled "The Principles of Jesus, the Guide to Peace and Happiness." Is it not more likely that God would choose the world's greatest moral teacher to demonstrate the victory of good over evil?

(4) Jesus inspired many of the most sweeping reforms in history, too, as we shall see. Might not God favor the world's greatest reformer? (With a miracle that led to further reforms?) After all, God promised Abraham that by his seed "all peoples of the World will be blessed."

(5) The "deeper magic" of the Resurrection is also hinted at outside of the Hebrew tradition. I have found many pointers to the Resurrection in Chinese culture, fulfilled by Christ. (I describe some of them in my longest academic work, *Fulfillment: A Christian Model of Religions*.)

(6) Lao Zi said that the *Tao* is on the side of the weak against powerful oppressors. Aslan came to life to defeat the White Witch and liberate Narnia from winter. Jesus was murdered by tyrants, backed by the Roman Empire. Would not raising an uncredentialed carpenter from the dead be a wonderful way of declaring victory for the oppressed? In *Christ and Caesar*, historian Will Du-

rant memorably tells that story: it even figures in an episode of *Star Trek*, echoing its centrality in real-life history.

News of the Resurrection comes as a shock, then. Death and decay seem so overwhelming, that it it hard to believe. But this shock makes more sense of life on deeper reflection, as it did for the first disciples.

So we can listen to debates over the Resurrection of Jesus without dismissing powerful historical evidence because it is "just too hard to believe." Who can say the flask of the world was not placed in the lab for this purpose? Of all the people about whom this story might be told, surely it is not mere coincidence that it is credibly told about Jesus.

Further Reading

Beginner: Many of William Lane Craig's debates on the Resurrection can be found on-line. Next chapter: please read *The Last Battle.*

Advanced: Aside from *Resurrection of the Son of God*, try Michael Licona, *The Resurrection of Jesus: A New Historiographical Approach*. Gary Habermas' work may be out by the time you read this. Timothy and Lydia McGrew offer a shorter but punchy seventy-page article entitled "The Argument From Miracles: A Cumulative Case for the Resurrection of Jesus of Nazareth." This can be found on-line, though Tim tells me the version in *The Blackwell Companion to Natural Theology* is definitive. On Jesus in Jewish prophecy, see Michael Brown. Lin Yutang tells his story, and the story of China, in *From Pagan to Christian*. On Christ and China, for a simpler version, and an introduction to China, see my *True Son of Heaven: How Jesus Fulfills the Chinese Culture*. On Ram Mohan Roy, see John Farquhar, *Modern Religious Movements in India*. I also refer again to Stephen Meyer's *The God Hypothesis* in this chapter.

NINE

Into Aslan's Shadow

"At a well in a yard they met a man who was beating a boy. The stick burst into flower in the man's hand. He tried to drop it, but it stuck to his hand. His arm became a branch, his body the trunk of a tree, his feet took root. The boy, who had been crying a moment before, burst out laughing and joined them." Prince Caspian

"The creatures came rushing…As they came right up to Aslan one or other of two things happened to each of them…You could see that (some) suddenly ceased to be Talking Beasts. They were just ordinary animals…I don't know what became of them. But the others looked at the face of Aslan and loved him…Eustace even recognized one of those very Dwarfs who had helped to shoot the horses." The Last Battle

Dogs break chains! Horses whinny and kick carts to bits! Susan and Lucy ride on a lion's back, while Bacchus and friends run alongside! A stone bridge is wrenched from its foundations! A school turns into a forest glade, and students scatter!

Has C. S. Lewis joined the hippie revolution? And why would a scholar and a gentleman laugh at a man who makes like a tree and leafs?

The story of that bloke echoes the *Bacchantes* by Euripides, a "weird" Greek drama, as the young Jack Lewis rightly called it. Dionysius or Bacchus was a figure of fun in *The Frogs*, a play by Aristophanes that won first prize in the Lenaia, a festival held in the god's honor in 405 BC. A few months later, *Bacchantes* won

First Prize in the larger City Dionysia competition, showing the god of parties in a very different mood.

The women of Thebes, just north of Athens, climbed the hills to worship him. Rumors of orgies came to the ears of Pentheus, the king. He banned worship of this wild god. Dionysius himself called on the king incognito, but Pentheus wouldn't listen or even speak politely. Finally the king went to spy on the wayward women, clambering up a pine tree for a box seat. Driven into a frenzy by the god, they ripped the tree down, and Pentheus limb from limb. His mother carried his head through the city, thinking she had slain a lion. Reason goes mad and is subject to gruesome punishment. Dionysius was the god of insanity as well as of wine, parties, and revelry.

What is so bloodthirsty a pagan god doing in an Anglican fairyland? And why, when Paul preached the Resurrection on Mars Hill, was the only convert a man named Dionysius?

Judgment is a recurring theme in Narnia. A cat loses her tongue. A girl forgets Narnia. A witch eats an apple and gains long life, but despair. A feast appears for dwarves in a stable, but they develop Covid tongue, tasting good food as straw and old turnips. A wizard thinks animals aim to eat him, when they only want to play Twenty Questions. ("Now, sir, are you animal, vegetable, or mineral?")

Even J. K. Rowling complained about Susan's fate. And did Lewis "kill off" his characters (as Pullman put it), to freeze them in a state of perpetual childhood?

Judgment may be the most difficult Christian doctrine. (As death is the most difficult human experience.) Not that the theme is absent from the fiction of Lewis' critics. Who does not rejoice when Mrs. Weasley shouts "Not my daughter, you bitch!" and blasts Bellatrix Lestrange?

Phillip Pullman offered what appears to be a faithful retelling of fifty Brothers Grimm tales in a 200th anniversary edition. Grimm is full of just, even ironic punishment. A wicked step-mother is made to put on red shoes and dance until she drops. A witch is burnt in the very oven in which she meant to bake two children. A wolf (no doubt a pup of Fenrir, the cosmic Wolf of Night) who had swallowed a grandmother and little girl, has his belly filled with rocks until he bursts. The Greeks also warned children that judgment may grow from the vices they indulge. Lie about wolves, and you may be eaten by one. Neglect to store up for winter, and you may go hungry.

Children thrill at judgment in fairy tales, much as the psalmist lustily calls Providence to smash his enemies' teeth in. In *Problem of Pain*, Lewis asks us to recognize the truth of this "savage" perspective. Consider a man who grows rich and powerful by laughing at the stupidity of those he destroys, sleeping like a baby, then betraying his accomplices and jeering at their bewilderment. Is it not better to be confronted with one's true nature and a sword, than to remain a satisfied dragon, swallowing lives, robbing treasures, and shedding fake tears?

"The trouble about making yourself stupider than you are is you very often succeed," Lewis noted of Uncle Andrew.

As in Greek drama and Grimm tales, there is irony to judgment in Lewis. "It was said afterwards that those particular boys were never seen again, but that there were a lot of very fine little pigs in that part of the country...."

Aslan does not turn children into pigs as an arbitrary punishment for their sins. Judgment is the bloom on the sin itself. The vices those boys nurtured—greed, materialism, small-mindedness, the meanness of many against one—flower into their natural, herdish form. "They have despised the Word of God. From them shall the word of man also be taken," shouts Merlin at the Bacchian banquet at the end of *That Hideous Strength*.

Similarly, Eustace made himself a dragon long before he visited Dragon Island. Recognizing his true form was the prerequisite of liberation from his reptilian form.

Not only animals, but humans, lose the gift of interpersonal communication: Rabadash, Andrew, the boys who turn into pigs. "The bolt of Tash falls from above!" Rabadash wagged his ears to terrify subordinates. Aslan gave him the more waggable ears of a donkey, so that those he oppressed in Tashbaan would smile, not cringe, at thought of their ruler. "Justice shall be mixed with mercy," Aslan promised: judgment first brought mercy to Rabadash's terrified subordinates, who deserved it more than he did.

Language, said novelist Tom Wolfe, created a new domain of life above plants and animals: the "Kingdom of Speech." Walker Percy agrees: something new entered the cosmos with "man's discovery of the sign." Judgment, then, consists in part of the natural consequences of refusing a gift one has been offered.

Rabadash echoes another old Greek story, *The Golden Ass* by Apuleius, which mixes farce with myth, magic, religion, and pornography. A witch turns a randy young man into a donkey, and he has many adventures trying to recover his human form. What Lewis called his best novel, *Till We Have Faces*, retells the story of Cupid and Psyche from that book, and also tells how the heroine "lost face" on the way to becoming (sister to Pinocchio) a "real girl."

The story of Susan is deeply troubling, yes, but mainly because Lewis lends her just what feminists demand: freedom to choose her path.

Susan Strolls into the Shadow

Peter: *"My sister Susan is no longer a friend of Narnia."*

Eustace: *"Yes. And whenever you've tried to get her to come and talk about Narnia or do anything about Narnia, she says, 'What wonder-*

ful memories you have! Fancy your still thinking about all those funny games we used to play when we were children!"

Jill: "Oh, Susan! She's interested in nothing nowadays except nylons and lipstick and invitation. She always was a jolly sight too keen on being grown-up."

Lady Polly: "Grown-up, indeed! I wish she would grow up. She wasted all her school time wanting to be the age she is now, and she'll waste all the rest of her life trying to stay that age." The Last Battle

J. K. Rowling summed up Susan's fate as follows: "There comes a point where Susan, who was the older girl, is lost to Narnia because she becomes interested in lipstick. She's become irreligious basically because she found sex. I have a big problem with that."

Pullman had a problem not only with Susan being "left behind," but with what he understood of the Christian take on life, death, and judgment, as revealed in the Narnia stories. "One of the most vile moments in the whole of children's literature," he said, comes when Aslan informs the children that they have died. Lewis "solves a narrative problem" by "slaughtering the lot" of his characters, Pullman puts it, then says they're better off dead! Pullman describes this as "propaganda in the service of a life-hating ideology," but "par for the course" for Lewis, for whom, "Death is better than life; boys are better than girls; light-colored people are better than dark-colored people; and so on."

Narnia is full of such "nauseating drivel," said Pullman, and Susan's fate is typical:

> Susan, like Cinderella, is undergoing a transition from one phase of her life to another. Lewis didn't approve of that. He didn't like women in general, or sexuality at all, at least at the stage in his life when he wrote the Narnia books. He was frightened and appalled at the notion of wanting to grow up.

Susan could have been the most interesting figure in the story, Pullman suggested elsewhere. But instead, she is "a Cinderella in a story where the Ugly Sisters win."

The claim that the Christian view of the afterlife reflects hatred of this one is not limited to critiques of children's books. In *Why I Am Not a Christian*, Bertrand Russell claimed that the Spanish used to baptize babies in the New World, then bash their brains out, concluding: "No orthodox Christian can find any logical reason for condemning their action." Murdering babies is clearly implied by the greater Christian attachment to the next life. (So there, pro-lifers and those who criticize Russell's own sordid seductions!)

Such manic critiques tell us more about the critic than about the person or belief criticized. What, the author of *Allegory of Love* and *Four Loves* gathered his skirts around him in horror at the thought of human reproduction? In *That Hideous Strength*, Venus settles over England to inspire hot women and handsome men, plus romantic bears and elephants. Mark Studdock's sin lies in dulling his passion for his wife with booze and ambition. "Love, Plato says, is the son of Want. Mark's body knew better than his mind had known till recently."

A famous Oxford playboy and theater critic, Kenneth Tynan, was planning a TV program on "Eroticism in the Arts." He suggested that his old tutor, C. S. Lewis, be interviewed to give the other side. The interviewer complained, "Oh, but he's just an old Christian apologist. We'll just get the straight Christian stuff." Tynan promised: "What you get will astonish you."

So it did. The interviewer asked: "Tell me, Lewis, why do you disapprove of the use of four-letter words in literature?"

"Because they are not erotic enough! They are not aphrodisiac enough. If you look through classical literature you will find that four-letter words are reserved for scurrility, satire, and abuse. These are not the emotions that we wish to feel, (do) we, when we are making love?" Tynan reports Lewis as replying.

The Chronicles of Narnia were written for younger children than *His Dark Materials* or even *Harry Potter*. (Though Marc Newman finds something creepy and dishonest in the way Pullman sexualizes twelve-year-olds in his stories, making their affairs just indirect enough to deny having done so.) Lewis excluded sex not only because his "target audience" was pre-pubescent, but because that form of sensuality was irrelevant to the themes he wished to explore.

As for the claim that Lewis hated life, in fact, his writings resoundingly echo God's verdict "It is good" upon Creation. Read his letters to children, accounts of romps across the English countryside with friends, or reports from his journey with Roger and June Green and his beloved wife Joy to Greece, as she was dying of cancer. In 1955, about when he was writing *The Last Battle*, Lewis sent a letter to Mary Van Deusen that reveals what a sunlight-hating underworld gnome he truly was:

> I am so glad that you are finding (as I do too) that life, far from getting dull and empty as one grows older, opens out. It is like being in a house where one keeps on discovering new rooms.

But death is a part of life, Forrest. Lewis often wished that it wasn't—read his accounts of the deaths of loved ones, beginning with his mother, and ending with the searing notebooks after his wife's passing (made into a movie which that dullard Anthony Hopkins largely spoiled), and tell me Lewis was blase about life or death. Literature, I often told my students, is about everything. From *Epic of Gilgamesh* on, death has been one of its great themes. Since Lewis believed in life after death, why shouldn't he try to depict it?

Lewis drew on Plato and Christian tradition to give us a glimpse of the afterlife. His essay "Transposition" explained the limitations of such sketches. A richer medium cannot fully reveal itself within a poorer medium. If a spoken language has fifty sounds, but its script only twenty-six letters, some need to do extra duty: the "t" for different sounds in "tank," "think" and "this," the "o" for "hot," "boat," and "boot," to give examples.

Lewis also tweaked Plato's "Allegory of the Cave" to explain the problem of describing the next world from within this one. In Lewis' version, a woman is imprisoned underground and gives birth to a child. She tries to help her boy understand Overworld, by drawing trees, flowers, and roads. But when she tells him that actually, the world does not consist of pencil marks at all, the child is deeply disillusioned! Images from this world may suggest, but cannot adequately portray, Aslan's Country.

Lord Digory says their experience of the New Narnia was "All in Plato," and "more like the real thing." (Odd that Pullman criticizes Lewis both for making everyone die, and for keeping Susan alive!) But Lewis could only use objects within our world to describe what is beyond it. So he is careful so say, in his preface to *The Great Divorce*, that he is not guessing what the afterlife is really like. Even an orange, he told a correspondent, is beyond guessing, if you have never tasted one: how much more eternal life!

Rowling and Pullman completely misread the story of Susan. Her problem wasn't sex or growing up: she had beaus in Narnia, as did Mr. and Mrs. Beaver, for that matter. And her "judgment" was not hell, it was that she missed out (for now) on what she purposely rejected: she was granted the grownup right to avoid a party she didn't wish to attend! (A right the young Jack Lewis would have died for.)

And so, for that matter, the animals that look at Aslan and hate him, enter the shadow willingly. They reject the gifts Aslan gives, such as reason and love. They limit themselves (at least for now) by their choices.

Susan, the Anti-Feminist

Susan's problem, Polly explains, is that she has not grown up enough. "Her idea is to race forward to the most foolish time of life, then stay there as long as one can." No boys are mentioned, just nylon, lipstick, and "invitations" (dates). Susan's actual fault was that of a pious woman Jesus met: she wasn't enough of a feminist!

"Blessed is the womb that bore you, and the breasts that gave you milk!"

"Blessed rather are those who hear the Word of God and obey it."

In most ancient civilizations, women were largely confined to the roles of consort and mother, that is, to reproduction. (Plus knitting and house management.)

Miracles, I argued, make us more human. Among Jesus' greatest miracles, as I will show in an upcoming book, was that he made the world (not just the West) see women as full human beings. (Even those who reduced themselves to breast, womb, or broom.) Matching, mating, and mothering had to come first in the ancient world, with its high infant mortality. But life is more than bread, or the energy that Pullman calls dust, and the Chinese call qi. Life originates in the deepest magic of all, self-sacrificial love. Susan painted herself into a corner: the hell of sensual reductionism into which Pullman is helping reduce the western world.

The Romans scattered body parts across their empire. We have become their disciples.

In *Sex Matters*, Mona Charen notes that drunkenness has increased, and female happiness decreased, even as sexual "freedoms" expand. "Romance and love, two of life's greatest joys, must begin with interest in the whole person," she argues. Lipstick and nylon are not "the whole person." Damnation, Lewis saw, means being imprisoned within ourselves. If lipstick can free us of the self—by using it to paint beauty, delight a lover, or dress up as a clown and make children laugh—then truck cases of the stuff to Susan's front door. In fact, when Jill Flewett, who stayed at the Lewis home (the Kilns) during the war (some say she was the model for Lucy), wished to act, Lewis helped pay for the training that launched her successful career! No doubt she wore lipstick and nylons on stage.

Confucius defined himself as a man so curious that he didn't notice the passage of time. Susan risked becoming a princess, a Mrs. Haversham, rather than a self-forgetful lover, mother, scientist, musician, grandmother, and follower of Christ—at least until the tragedy of the railroad accident.

As often happens in adolescence, "growing up" narrowed Susan's world. Edmund was tempted by greed, Eustace by social nihilism, Mark Studdock by the lure of the "inner ring," Frodo by a golden ring. As the singer Mark Heard put it, "You're not in love, not even with your lovers." For a while, Susan became a "material girl," neglecting not only her "first love," but all "I-Thou" relationships.

Susan was not yet a witch or balrog, though. Her character was still in flux. Lewis told Pauline Bannister in a letter, "I have a feeling that the story of her journey would be longer and more like a grownup novel than I wanted to write," suggesting that Pauline write it herself.

Yet Susan's fate does sound a warning. Boromir was seduced by the ring but repented and died a good death. No Potter hero fell so low: in that sense, Rowling's fantasy was less bold, true to life, or "grown up" than that of Lewis, Tolkien, or the Brothers Grimm. (Though she pulled no punches in her adult novel, *Casual Vacancy*.)

The Shoddy Lands

One of Lewis' lesser-known short stories shows that in the tale of Susan, he was also warning himself.

A former student (the story goes) came to visit Lewis with his girlfriend. During the visit, Lewis nodded off, and found himself strolling through the girl's subconscious. Most objects in that land seemed dreary: trees were vague blurs, most flowers were smudges, people were indistinct. (Ray Bradbury's *Fahrenheit 451* gives a similar picture of damnation by mass vulgarity.) But here and there something stood out: fashionable women's clothing, the faces of certain men. The girl's own figure rose like a giantess preening in front of a mirror. Two sounds were barely audible: her boyfriend knocking to be let into her world, and the deeper, quieter call of Christ.

Waking, Lewis felt sorry for the boyfriend, but also worried lest anyone tour his psyche.

"Then we shall know, even as we are known." Stripping off masks and revealing our true faces has been the job of the novelist since Christ came into this world. (Augustine's *Confessions* was the prototype.)

Sheep and Goats

At the end of time, Jesus said, the nations would be gathered for judgment. The Son of Man would separate people, as a shepherd separates sheep and goats. The sheep would be welcomed to "take your inheritance," the kingdom "prepared for you since the creation of the world . . . For I was hungry and you gave me something to eat, I was thirsty and you gave me something to drink, I was a stranger and you invited me in, I needed clothes and you clothed me, I was sick and you looked after me, I was in prison and you came to visit me."

The goats, who ignored those in need, were not sent to their proper homes, but to "eternal fire prepared for the devil and his angels."

The sheep did not love others to "gain salvation," but because Christian salvation implies becoming Christ-like: that is what the word means.

C. S. Lewis was an orthodox Christian. He believed in miracles, the Resurrection, God's judgment, and life after death. He insisted that the door to hell was locked from the inside, quoting Milton's famous line, "Better to reign in hell, than serve in heaven."

In *The Problem of Pain*, Lewis noted that Jesus speaks of hell in three ways: as lasting punishment, destruction, and privation or exclusion. These are not meant to be literal descriptions. After all, if hell is "outer darkness," how could it also be flames? Physical flames create light. And how can suffering last if one is destroyed? The image of hell Lewis gave in *The Great Divorce* is of an endless, drizzly suburb, from which you could take a bus to heaven if you liked, and even find redemption. Following the vision of that book, the psychologist Scott Peck pictured the Afterlife as a kind of hospital for souls. For Lewis, salvation meant turning away from the self, first perhaps to Truth or Beauty, but ultimately to God.

The head of NICE chose self-worship, instead:

> The taste for the Other, that is, the very capacity for enjoying good, is quenched in him except in so far as his body still draws him into some rudimentary contact with the outside world. Death removes this last contact. He has his last wish—to live wholly in the self, and make the best of what he finds there. And what he finds there is Hell.

Lewis did not describe the concrete reality of Aslan's shadow. It is the land of unreality. Lewis sought Heaven not out of contempt for this world, but because his faith added meaning and hope to the hints of eternity he found in the English countryside, in literature, and in his many friendships.

Further Reading

Beginning: Lewis: *The Problem of Pain* contains a chapter or two on hell. *The Great Divorce* is a quick but profound read. I also recommend Don Richardson's *Heaven Wins: Heaven, Hell, and the Hope of Every Person*. Next chapter: please read *The Horse and His Boy* and *The Last Battle*.

Intermediate: Lewis: *Till We Have Faces*. Scott Peck's *People of the Lie* is interesting, taken with an occasional grain of salt. Mona Charen's *Sex Matters* is good to read alongside Heather MacDonald's *The War on Cops*, which together show the hell that failure to discipline sexuality creates. (Also an occasional theme of *the Inferno* by Dante, whom Lewis loved.) I also refer to the second of Marc Newman's excellent essays at *The Catholic Exchange* critiquing Pullman, "The Golden Compass: Sexualizing Children in the World of His Dark Materials." The first is entitled "*The Golden Compass* Brings Nietzsche to Narnia: The Philosophical Underpinnings of *His Dark Materials.*" Bertrand Russell's ideas can be found in *Why I Am Not a Christian*, and his story, in his autobiography.

TEN

Tash vs. Aslan

"But do you think," said Lucy, "Aslan's country would be that sort of country—I mean, the sort you could ever sail to?"

"I do not know, madam,' said Reepicheep. "But there is this. When I was in my cradle, a wood woman, a Dryad, spoke this verse over me:

"Where sky and water meet,
Where the waves grow sweet
Doubt not, Reepicheep,
To find all you seek
There is the utter east." Voyage of the Dawn Treader

Warnie Lewis shipped off to the "utter east" in 1927, serving the British empire in Hong Kong, Shanghai, and Shandong Province. He wrote his younger brother critical descriptions of China. Just then, Jack Lewis was trying to map faiths in relation to one another. Can one get to Aslan's Country by sailing east?

I arrived at Kai Tak Airport in the British colony of Hong Kong in January, 1984. In the summer, after a Christian training program in a former hospital once occupied by the Japanese above Central on Hong Kong Island, I traveled China by train in search of my own answers.

China didn't look like Aslan's Country. Three great "pagan" religions had (it was said) long dominated her culture: Confucianism, Taoism, and Buddhism. Then China was conquered by the People's Liberation Army under the communist dictator, Mao Zedong. Chairman Mao squashed Chinese religions, along with the few foreign churches that dotted the landscape. He created a Narnia where it was always winter (sterilized by concrete not snow), and few celebrated the birth of Buddha, Confucius, or Lao Zi, still less Jesus of Nazareth.

I took a hard seat north to Beijing, with people sleeping on cardboard on the floor, sharing *longyan* fruit with me, or playing cards and smoking Winstons through the night. I found a hotel south of the inner city, past a canal where fishermen still dipped nets, and beyond which horse carts were not allowed.

The deep blue tiles of the Altar of Heaven beckoned me on the horizon. I walked miles to find an entrance. Within this grand rectangular oasis, evergreens shaded cool morning grass. Old people practiced *tai qi* or fan dances, young people played badminton, and birds sung in cages hanging from trees.

The Altar of Prayer for a Good Harvest, the centerpiece of the park, took my breath away. The cypress guarding the gates looked like the western red cedars of our Northwest shrunken to the size but also dignity of ents. Three circular roofs with blue tiles, like layers of a cake, rose one above the other to meet the summer sky. (This was before anyone owned a car, so the sky was also blue.) Lin Yutang called the altar "the most beautiful single piece of creation in all China."

The emperor came here once a year to pray for a good harvest to *Shang Di*, "Ruler Above." Thirty years after Columbus landed in America, the most magnificent building in China was erected to revive ancient customs, a faith found in the oldest Chinese texts, the *Book of History* and the *Book of Poetry*, which along with the *Yi Jing* made up Confucius' Old Testament.

Nothing should have been more alien to a naïve young Presbyterian from Seattle than this hoary temple, where rites rooted in beliefs from before the birth of Christ were carried into the early 20th Century. Yet I felt as Reepicheep did when he plunged into the eastern sea and tasted the sweet waters of the "utter east" promised in the Dryad's song.

Who was this "Huang Tian Shang Di," "Awesome Heavenly Ruler Above," whom China's emperor came to worship? Might that be another name for "God?" So claimed missionary Don Richardson in a book I had been reading, *Eternity in Their Hearts*.

The building contained no idols. Four red and gold pillars, representing the seasons, and twelve red pillars, representing the months, then twelve more in the walls, rose in concentric circles, supporting the structure's central vault.

Aslan sometimes hides messages in monuments over ancient cities, we learn in *The Silver Chair*. The red and gold pillars reminded me of four gospels, the words of Jesus marked in red, tinged with gold edging.

St. Paul described Christians as "pillars" in the temple of God. According to Exodus, Moses sprinkled blood over twelve stone pillars, representing the tribes of Israel. Jesus called twelve apostles to represent those tribes. (Often just called "The Twelve" in the gospels.) Sacrifice was held in both the Jewish temple and the Chinese complex. So I saw in this altar, with its four red and gold and twelve visible and twelve more hidden pillars, where the emperor came to worship the "Awesome Heavenly Ruler Above," a message all the more powerful for the exotic garb in which it was dressed. "To stand in the presence of God (like those red pillars), one must be sprinkled with the blood of Christ."

It felt as if Someone were asking: "Do you think I just came here with the western missionaries? I have been here all along. I made China."

Thus my life-long journey to the "utter east" began. I hiked China's mountains, waded her rivers, interviewed worshipers in temples and students in classrooms. I studied modern and ancient Chinese, coming to love the nation's great novels, philosophers, and poets. I wrote about China for many magazines. I described the connections I found in my first book, *True Son of Heaven: How Jesus Fulfills the Chinese Culture*, then years later, expanded and defended my arguments in a doctoral dissertation.

Unlike Reepicheep, I was not the first to reach Aslan's Country by traveling to our Far East. In 635 AD, a Christian monk named Alopen passed through Central Asian deserts to the ancient capital of Chang An (Xian), where the emperor worshiped *Shang Di* at an older Altar of Heaven. (Which now overlooks a soccer field down an obscure ally.) The Tai Zong emperor, one of the greatest rulers in China's long history, welcomed Alopen with courtesy and curiosity. In 781, a Persian Christian named Jing Jing wrote the story of that first meeting of China and Christ on a memorial stone, which was dug up 800 years later, and can now be viewed in the Confucian temple in downtown Xian, on your left as you enter the Forest of Steles. In it, Tai Zong recommends the new faith as "purely excellent and natural...beneficial to all creatures." Jing Jing says Christians did not practice slavery, and names a series of Chinese kings and Christian apostles, both of whom he calls *Sheng*, or "sages." East and West meet on that stone, joining the stories of two great civilizations.

About the time that stele was dug up, the brilliant Italian Jesuit, Matteo Ricci, astounded China's literati with remarkable feats of memory. Ricci wrote a best-seller on friendship, and dove into a swollen river to save the family of a mandarin friend. He studied China's oldest records, and announced that the ancient Chinese had worshipped the true God. Xu Guangqi, whose agricultural encyclopedia is described as a scientific landmark in modern high school texts, agreed, arguing that ancient terms like "True Ruler" and "Sovereign" also referred to God.

In the 19th Century, James Legge, probably the greatest western student of Chinese religions, gathered with friends at the Altar of Heaven and sang, hand in hand, "Praise God from whom all blessings flow." Legge also said he heard a Voice there, telling him to take his shoes off before entering, for "the place whereon you stand is holy ground." In the mid-20th Century, Lin Yutang wrote a novel in exile describing how the communists were destroying China, but slipping a joyful thought about the "Temple of Heaven at moonlight" into the mind of the English hero who steals into China to save his girlfriend from Mao's collectives. Lin also wrote a combined autobiography and spiritual history of China which introduced Jesus with the ancient phrase, "Blow out the candles, the sun has risen!"

Five years after my visit to the Altar of Heaven, the Democracy Movement broke out a few miles to the north, and the state gunned down hundreds of students in the name of its ideology. One of the movement's leaders, Yuan Zhiming, escaped China on a motor-boat, as he told me later. Yuan began reading the Bible and Lao Zi, and also found a path to Aslan's country through the ancient philosophy of the nation he called "the Divine Land."

How does Christianity relate to other faiths? C. S. Lewis helped crack the code, preparing me for what I found in China. Parts of his formula can be found in Narnia.

Tashlan Strikes Back

Lewis became a Christian following a late-night stroll along Addison's Walk in Magdalen College with J. R. R. Tolkien and Hugh Dyson, talking about how Christianity relates to other faiths: "We began on metaphor and myth—interrupted by a rush of wind which came so suddenly on the still, warm evening and sent so many leaves pattering down that we thought it was raining."

Lewis loved Greek, Celtic, and Norse mythologies. It was from the distant fenns of fairyland that the voice of his deepest desire called. But he felt, as the Chinese philosopher Feng Yulan put it, "Among philosophical theories, it is a general rule that those that can be loved cannot be believed, and those that can be believed cannot be loved." Lewis was, after all, a veteran of those cruel French foxholes. And already with his mother's death he felt he had left behind "all settled happiness."

Lewis' friends persuaded him that the believable and the lovable might reconcile in Christ. "Now the story of Christ is simply a true myth: a myth working on us in the same way as the others, but with this tremendous difference that it really happened."

Jesus told his disciples: "Do not think I have come to do away with the Law and the Prophets. I have not come to abolish, but to fulfill." With the help of Tolkien and Dyson, Lewis came to believe that Jesus fulfilled not only Old Testament prophecies, but truths he loved within Gentile mythologies as well.

It is often said religions fit together in one of three ways: "pluralism," "exclusivism," or "inclusivism." Religions, said pluralist John Hick, are like planets circling a sun, which at first he called "God," then more vaguely, "the Real." But Hick never explained what deep truths he found in Aztec human sacrifice, or how much divine sunlight shone on whatever faith planet the Gestapo occupied. In fact, he admitted his "Real" has to remain neutral between good and evil. In *Fulfillment: A Christian Model of Religions*, I also ask what "exclusivism" can mean when it comes to Truth. Confronted with the beauty of Stoic morality or a story of the bodhisattva Guan Yin showing compassion for lost souls, even "exclusivists" admit there is some truth in other traditions. So what do they exclude? Error? Everyone claims to cast that off.

That night on Addison's walk, an alternative model that goes back to St. Paul, or even to Jesus' words about "fulfilling" the Law and the Prophets, came to life in Lewis' mind. I believe this concept can help us crack one of the great puzzles of our interlocking and mutually-irritating world: how East and West can meet without blowing each other up.

What Is Fulfillment?

Both the Greek word *plerou* and the English word *fulfill* originally referred to the act of filling something up, like a cup with wine. That act implies six elements, which also describe how Christ relates to other faiths, as Aslan helps illustrate:

1. A story, or sequence of events. A cup is empty, liquid fills it, you drink.

The Chronicles of Narnia are seven tales about children who find a land ruled by a lion who tells them they may come to "know me better in your world." The story transcends not only history, but biology: it includes fauns, beavers, centaurs, owls, marshwiggles, eagles, bears, and mice, plus Aslan singing stars into being, then calling them to fall on Narnia's last day. And like the Nestorian stele, Lewis' tales join two worlds—England and Narnia—into a bigger story, what post-modernists deride as a "*metanarrative.*"

Digory and Polly also discover a "Wood between the Worlds," from which one can travel to many other planets. They find that even the cursed world of Charn is not strange to Aslan.

Many think Christian missionaries go to alien lands to end local songs, since "paganism" is from the devil. And in the flush of western power, some missionaries did chop down totem poles or stop clan dances. But others heard the words "I have been here all along," and found doors into Aslan's Country from the back of many altars to Heaven.

Abraham was told that through his seed, all nations would be blessed. How could the beleaguered and truculent Jews see their kin as the vehicle through whom the *goyim* would prosper? But read the Old Testament carefully, and you find that promise repeated hundreds of times: God will bless all nations, through Abraham's descendants.

When St. Paul preached on Mars Hill, in a few words he united the Greco-Roman story to that ancient Jewish salvation narrative.

Thinkers like Socrates, Plato, and Cleanthes had grown dissatisfied with their own poets and playwrights, thrilling as their stories were. Philosophers wanted "truth that can be believed." They began praying to a God who guided "the whole universe" and "established all the works of creation" and Reason itself, as the Stoic Cleanthes put it. "From you we have our being."

Paul quoted two Greek philosophers who spoke of God that way, Epimenides and Aratus. He cited a famous, enigmatic altar on a hillside nearby which had been dedicated "to an unknown God." We don't know all that he said about Jesus, but he could have portrayed him as a civil patriot who, as Plato foretold, drank an even more bitter cup than Socrates drained. According to the great playwright Aeschylus, the Trojan War ended on Mars Hill, in a trial at which Apollo warned, "There is no resurrection." Paul rebutted Apollo, by dramatically announcing: "God has raised (Jesus) from the dead."

Rumor spread out like ripples in the pool of the Hermit of the Southern March, from Jerusalem to Athens, Alexandria, and Addis Ababa, then "the uttermost parts of the world." In Nordic lands, India, Africa, and China, the "new story" of Jesus seemed rooted in the oldest and most sacred traditions, like a wardrobe built of a local apple tree that led to a distant world. The pious Lutheran Wilhelm Grimm paid tribute to that heritage when he had an owl, a raven, and a dove perch on a tree above Snow White's grave. These birds represented Greek, Nordic, and Jewish wisdom. They were, said Ronald Murphy, "the soul of mankind keeping watch over her body to see if it can come to life again." The Prince loved Snow White and gave her new life, uniting the dreams of many peoples, represented by those three birds. Wherever the story of Jesus goes, it solders together the most sacred tales of many lands into a single human story.

2. (*Dialectic*) But what about Tash? Didn't Lewis dismiss the great empire that dominated Narnia as the land of the bird-demon? Surely this is an ugly portrait of pagan religion:

> At a first glance you might have mistaken it for smoke, for it was grey and you could see things through it. But the deathly smell was not the smell of smoke. Also, this thing kept its shape instead of billowing and curling as smoke would have done. It was roughly the shape of a man but it had the head of a bird; some bird of prey with a cruel, curving beak. It had four arms which it held high above its head, stretching them out Northward as if it wanted to snatch all Narnia in its grip; and its fingers—all twenty of them—were curved like its beak and had long, pointed, bird-like claws instead of nails. It floated on the grass instead of walking, and the grass seemed to wither beneath it.

Before filling a mug, one must empty it. Shake oats and old oregano out. Scrub yesterday's dried cocoa, rinse, and only then pour in your morning beverage.

Our souls, too, need to be cleansed before filling again.

Aravis loses her faith in Tash before she meets Aslan. Emeth arrives in what he takes for Tash's country, finding a lion instead of a ghostly buzzard. But he had already rejected cruel stories about Tash, as Plato rejected the notion that the "real Zeus" would act like the randy thunder god in Homer's *Iliad* or Hesiod's *Theogony*.

No history that ignores religious evil is credible. John Hick forgot the rain god Tlaloc in Mexico, who demanded that children be tortured to death so their tears might bring rain. He also ignored Mohammed's warning to his wives that Allah would heat the flames of hell hotter for them if they complained when the prophet dragged his foster son's beautiful Ex into his harem.

Lewis loved myths, and read philosophers like Plato and Confucius with reverence. No one needed to tell him that other religions contain beauty and truth: those beauties were precisely what led him to Christ.

But an honest theory of religions must take the "dark side" of religion into account. It must not worship a donkey with a lion suit that appears as a silhouette in the flickering light of a bonfire, like John Hick's equally shadowy "Real."

As much as he loved Baldur and Odysseus, Lewis knew that Calormen was, in some ways, a truer picture of ancient civilization. He saw Hinduism as the chief rival to Christianity, and Buddhism and Islam as knock-offs of those two. But in India, he noted, exalted philosophy existed side-by-side with temple prostitution, and girls were burnt to death on their husband's pyre. In *Reflections on the Psalms*, Lewis suggested that the Jews loved the Law so passionately because its "rightness" or "fittingness" contrasted not with Homer or Plato, but with the "systematic cruelty" of the Assyrians with their "appalling deities," and with the "sacred prostitution, sacred sodomy, and babies thrown into the fire for Moloch" of their Phoenician neighbors. Assyrian and Phoenician gods were undeniably Tash-like.

On my first visit to Beijing, I also visited Tiananmen Square, across Chang An Avenue from the Forbidden City. Citizens would be gunned down during demonstrations that erupted there five years later. An obelisk memorializing earlier generations of "martyrs" still rises 124 feet above the square. On that monument, Mao's words are inscribed:

> Eternal glory to the heroes of the people who from 1840 laid down their lives in the many struggles against domestic and foreign enemies and for national independence and the freedom and well-being of the people!

This is China's Stone Table, where Jadis' blade slashed, heroes died, and then died again.

The theme goes back to King Tang, founder of the Shang Dynasty, millennia before Christ. When a famine or a drought struck, King Tang insisted that he be the sacrifice: "When guilt is found anywhere in you who occupy the myriad regions, let it rest on me, the One man," as James Legge translated the "Announcement of Tang" in the *Book of History*.

The last king of Narnia echoed the first king of the Shang: "Let me be killed. I ask nothing for myself. But come and save all Narnia."

Christ's death on the cross fulfills the pattern of the Straight and the Crooked. The cross is dialectic. Good (Aslan) meets evil (Witch), producing richer good. As grapes foment into wine, so the cross redeems lynching into love. Jordan Peterson admitted, "For our own good, we all need a glimpse of the Evil Queen." At the death of Aslan, we meet that Evil Queen, and shake her out of our lives.

(3) Intent (*Telos*). Flasks are designed for experiments, and purposefully filled with media and reactive elements. Pouring wine into a cup is also a deliberate act. Particles of old food, which may contain botulism or other germs, are first washed out. Molecules do not collide and splash a bottle of Pinot Noir up onto your table by accident. It takes labor and planning to grow, harvest, mash, ferment, bottle, and age wine. Someone must also manufacture

the drinking vessel with much care. Similarly, Puddleglum and his two English companions find signs within foreign cultures (Narnian, giant, and Underworld) because a lion-without-borders is plotting to save a prince.

In *Reflections on the Psalms*, Lewis told of a Roman bathhouse in which a customer complained how tepid the water was. An attendant replied, "It'll be hotter soon." Later that day, a fire broke out. Perhaps the "coincidence" between the slave's remarks, and the fire, was accidental. Or maybe the attendant had been plotting arson.

Was it a "coincidence" that Plato foresaw the noblest man as being, in effect, crucified? Lewis viewed Plato's insight as more significant than the "lucky guess" of the attendant. As a "surpassing theological genius," Plato foresaw what often happens when the likes of Aslan and the White Witch, the "Straight" and the "Crooked," "cross" paths.

If God plans history, the Dryad who whispered into Reepicheep's velvety baby ear was not just guessing, like a carnival gypsy or even a theological genius. The noble mouse was meant to find Aslan's Country. Telling his own story in *Surprised by Joy*, Lewis also saw divine planning in such conversions: "A young man who wishes to remain a sound Atheist cannot be too careful of his reading. There are traps everywhere—'Bibles laid open, millions of surprises,' as Herbert says, '*fine nets and stratagems*.'"

Why shouldn't James Legge or I hear a Voice at the Altar of Heaven? Early Christians heard it in the prophets, Passover, and the passion of the Suffering Servant. When Daniel said "the Messiah" would make an "end to sin" (in seventy weeks = 490 years), he seemed to time salvation to the ministry of Jesus. The last chapter of Mencius predicts a new sage every 500 years, which counting from the death of Confucius, who Mencius saw as China's greatest sage, also brings us to about when a young rabbi rose dripping from the Jordan River. Augustine found Christ in the religious history of Rome. Don Richardson saw divine planning in the legend of the Peace Child, which transformed the treacherous Sawi of New Guinea. Even Will Durant was astounded at how Norse beliefs seemed front-loaded for Christian conversion:

> In this twilight of the Gods all the universe fell to ruin: not merely sun and planets and stars, but, at last, Valhalla itself, and all its warriors and deities: only Hope survived—that in the slow movement of time a new earth would form, a new heaven, a better justice, and a higher god than Odin or Thor. Perhaps that mighty fable symbolized the victory of Christianity... Or had the Viking poets come to doubt—and bury—their gods?

Odin died on a tree. A Christian from the "Dark Ages" told the story of the tree on which a greater Odin died, in a gorgeous poem called *Dream of the Rood*.

> On me the Son of God once suffered; therefore now
> I tower mightily underneath the heavens...
> And I may heal all those in awe of me.
> Once I became the cruelest of tortures,
> Most hateful to all nations, till the time
> I opened the right way of life for men."

Read Ronald Murphy's account of the Viking Sacred Ash or John Farquhar's histories of Indian religion with Christ at the center. Note how God is spoken of in the *Romance of the Three Kingdoms*. Walk through Chinese villages and read spring couplets on pagan doorways that seemed to call for a Resurrection.

After years of meeting Aslan in such unexpected places, the story of human culture often grows to look like a redemptive plot.

4. Apologetic

"If you are thirsty, come and drink!"

A beverage should pass the "sniff test" before you put it in your mouth. Look! Shake! Rap! Stick out your tongue! A vessel might contain deadly hemlock or life-giving wine. Faith is only reasonable when tested by senses and mind: memory, conscience, intuition, imagination, critical analysis.

Fulfillment supports the truth of Christianity in two ways. First, some prophesies seem to cry out like stones. When Jewish doctor and Holocaust survivor Vera Schlamm read the "Suffering Servant" passage of Isaiah 53 she wrote, "It seemed so obvious that it was talking about Jesus that I thought, 'Well, this is a Christian translation.'" But the Jewish translation still reminded her of Jesus.

Such "aha" moments, like opening a window and seeing "Under Me," occur on Mars Hill and at the Altar of Heaven, or when confronted with the Nordic Yggsdrassil or the Sawi Peace Child. "Look! Look! Look! The Lion! Aslan himself!" as Lucy put it.

But other such "moments" may occur over years, when vast platelets of experience slowly grind together, and redemptive patterns of history become visible from the window after a winter rain.

5. Synthesis

To make wine, add a fermenting agent and water to grapes, yielding a mix of alcohol, fruit sugars, and the grape's own flavors and life-enhancing chemicals. To make cocoa, mix chocolate, sugar, cream, and boiling water.

Truth must meet the nutritional needs (Jesus said) of "mind, soul, heart, and strength." Scholar of religions James Thrower argued that a good theory should not make us pick one vision and just toss the rest in the garbage bin.

> The implication is rather that any naturalistic theory which stands
> a chance of winning support today will have to find a way of com-

bining the insights of Marx, Freud, Nietzsche, Durkheim, Weber, and a host of others besides, just as any theory which seeks to substantiate the claims of religion to be a valid response to transcendent reality will have to combine insights from a number of differing religious traditions.

Students of physics seek a "unified theory," a formula that explains how the four physical forces fit together. Astronomers tell a "universal story" of how all galaxies spread out from an original "Big Bang." By synthesizing, or joining, the stories of many cultures (a truer form of what is called "diversity" and "inclusion"), the Gospel satisfies both mind and intuition. Since first visiting the Altar of Heaven, I long to sketch more of the grand story of how Christ joins diverse traditions: at the end of the chapter, I will name other authors with a similar vision.

One reason J. R. R. Tolkien found Narnia irritating was because Lewis stuffed so much into it, making it messy, like Harry Potter's Room of Requirement. Peter Rabbit-like talking animals. Greek river-gods, divine stars, and talking trees. Nordic dwarves. Sherlock Holmes is mentioned as an historical figure. Father Christmas even pops in, passing around what look suspiciously like "Gifts of the Spirit" that the Apostle Paul wrote about.

But this is where A.N. Wilson's suggestion that Lewis retreated from the complexity of adult debate falls wide of the mark. Lewis became a Christian because he saw, like Einstein, that images are tools of reason, by which we try (among other things) to fit distinct facts into one coherent model. Narnia is a thought-experiment, meant to answer a question Lewis had asked all his life: how truth and fancy fit together.

As a young teacher, Lewis read G. K. Chesterton's *Everlasting Man* and, he says, "saw the whole Christian outline of history set out in a form that seemed to me to make sense."

Chesterton thought "the experts" explained faiths wrongly. It is misleading to speak of "world religions" like Buddhism, Christianity, Confucianism, Hinduism, Islam, and Taoism. Just as many organic molecules are formed from elements you can count on one hand (carbon, hydrogen, oxygen, nitrogen, sometimes a little phosphorus), so "great religious traditions" are made of just a few elements the world over: God, gods, devils, and philosophy.

People often speak of "Judeo-Christian" or "Abrahamic" religions that worship one Creator God. But Chesterton had read Andrew Lang's *The Making of Religion*, which introduced the idea that primitive peoples worldwide were often theists. Students of early cultures like Wilhelm Schmidt, Paul Radin, Mircea Eliade, and Win Corduan, have since discovered faith in One God in many primitive cultures.

China never fully lost that ancient faith. (Though it was often obscured.) At the Altar of Heaven, the Chinese ignored "new-fangled" religions like Taoism and Buddhism to worship the God of their remote ancestors. One hears echoes of primitive theism even in great novels like *Romance of Three Kingdoms*. Not even the Cultural Revolution erased memory of *Shang Di*: the works of the Nobel-Prize winning former soldier, Mo Yan, often refer to God by various names.

But anthropologists often find the purest theism among primitive tribes. Narnia was a little land, like Israel, that had to fend off the armies of a great empire, Calormen. In *Discovery of God*, Rodney Stark showed that most primitive tribes were aware of a Supreme God, especially nomadic peoples. But as Win Corduan told me, "There's not a lot of cash value to (theism)." Great empires tended to be hierarchical, like Calormen, and priests created gods for a wealthy clientele in the image of animals and men. One can also flatter Caesar by calling him a god. But the hummingbird loses its charm when it becomes a blood-thirsty Aztec deity, and once worshipped, humans often also become devils.

Chesterton's four elements combine in the Gospel story. The *Creator* of time and space comes with whiskers and tail, or hands that bleed (as in a *myth*). On the cross (or Stone Table), he confronts the *powers of darkness*. And because the story of Jesus is historical, *philosophers* who "seek the truth of things," as Chesterton put it, can like the bear who spots a well-laden fruit tree in Aslan's Country, waddle over and sink their teeth into sweet fact-hood.

The Gospel thus unites philosophers, story-tellers, seekers after God, and those who beg liberation from powers of darkness. It also unifies peoples, as Liu Ning said the cross did, reaching out to embrace nations, and strata within them.

A Nineteenth Century observer compared China to a pile of loose sand. Literati had little to do with peasants. The rice-growing South and the wheat-growing North did not easily meet. Mountain bandits raided the plains, and minorities fought to be free, with bands speaking five different languages within a few miles of ridges and valleys (as one still finds in Jinping County on the border of Vietnam). Yuan Zhiming, one of the leaders of the Democracy Movement, would later write in my anthology, *Faith Seeking Understanding*: "I believe that if these ancient sages—Lao Zi, Confucius, Mozi, Zhuang Zi, Mencius—were to meet Jesus, they would declare Jesus to be Lord." I agree. East is East, and West is West? No, East was never one, nor was West, until they found unity within themselves, and with each other, under God. In Christ alone do male and female, Greek, Jew, Miao, and Han, professor and truck driver, become one. Again, see the end of the chapter to explore this exciting secret history in detail.

6. (*Reform*) Finally, the contents of the cup do one good, like that last drink before the Calormenes close in, or the spring rising

from the lion's footsteps. Wine quenches thirst, or helps you celebrate with friends. Its flavonoids strengthen your heart. Alcohol converts to sugar, and boosts your energy.

Wrong will be right, when Aslan comes in sight
At the sound of his roar, sorrows will be no more,
When he bares his teeth, winter meets its death
And when he shakes his mane, we shall have winter again.

Patches of green grow. Mist turns to white to gold then fades. Light shines through the forest and the heavens appear. Travelers cross gushing melt-water. Celandines spring up under silver birches. Thrushes sing, quarrel, and tidy their feathers. Bees buzz. The scent of hawthorns and currant overpower the walkers.

The Gospel does not respond to "other faiths" with a simple "Nein!" Nor a simple "Si, amigo!" It does not simply exclude, include, or set faiths in a row like fruits in tropical market.

Faced with world religions, the Gospel thus accomplishes six impossible things before breakfast: joins all stories, brings good from evil, draws meaning from "signs" around us, satisfies our thirst for truth, unites tribes, and makes the world better. The cup is thus filled. "To life!" Drink up!

Phillip Pullman dislikes the Christian story, on the contrary, because he thinks the drink it offers is bitter and life-denying. For one thing, he thinks Aslan is a roadblock to the justice that modern humans should seek.

The Chronicles of Narnia touch repeatedly on "social justice" issues: race, slavery, the role of women. As one who fought sex trafficking in Asia as a young man, whose brother is a police officer, and who explored Capitol Hill Autonomous Zone (CHAZ) in the summer of 2020 with concern, this question also lies close to my heart.

Lewis did not offer detailed solutions to problems that would roil the western world sixty years later. But as the frozen stone figures in the White Witch's castle would discover, Aslan is the ultimate "social justice warrior."

So let us gather a symposium, or lynch mob as the night deepens, on a hill above downtown Seattle to decide the fate of the *Chronicles of Narnia*. (And of western society.) Robin DiAngelo, who took her BA a few blocks south at Seattle University, has waved her usual high fee to join us. "Anti-Racist" scholar Ibram Kendi flew in from Boston. Pullman arrived on that flight we looked in on earlier, from London. (J. K. Rowling arrived two days earlier.) A crowd has gathered to decide whether literature by the famous "dead white male" should be placed in the hands of vulnerable children, or canceled. A bonfire has been lit. A hobo with a donkey is selling wine by a small tent city. Rowling is in hot water already due to insensitive remarks about transsexuals, and had best watch her tongue.

Who will speak for the defense? I see you, sir, with the wispy white beard. Are you a lawyer? Oh, a professor! Well step on up, if you dare!

Further Reading

Beginners: Read Acts 17: 16-32. Also try Don Richardson's *Peace Child* and *Eternity in Their Hearts*, along with my *True Son of Heaven: How Jesus Fulfills the Chinese Culture*, and also *How Jesus Passes the Outsider Test for Faith: The Inside Story*. The chapters in *Faith Seeking Understanding* on Christ and Culture by Miriam Adeney, Ivan Satyavrata, Yuan Zhiming, and my interview with Don Richardson, are also quite readable, I think. You may also like to listen to my interview of Win Corduan online.

Advanced: Original texts are usually best. There are so many worth reading on this subject, though (Justin Martyr, Clement,

Augustine, Ricci, Xu, Lin Yutang, The Brothers Grimm, Roberto De Nobili, Alexander De Rhodes, Jing Jing, Yuan Zhiming) that some readers may prefer to start with introductory works. For Africa, try John Mbiti (though some say he exaggerates a bit), Lamin Sanneh, and Kwame Bediako. For India, John Farquhar and Ivan Satyavrata: Mangalwadi's *The World of Gurus* is also fascinating. For China, Lin's *From Pagan to Christian*, and my *True Son of Heaven: How Jesus Fulfills the Chinese Culture*, will get you started. Peter Phan's work on Roberto De Nobili in Vietnam also contains fascinating nuggets.

To go deeper on both the philosophy of fulfillment, and the history of such ideas in China, try my *Fulfillment: A Christian Model of Religions*, which also introduces many other works. A fascinating early defense of a similar if simpler Christian model, can be found in *Adaptation*, by the Jesuit missionary to India, Roberto De Nobili.

On God and primitive man, see Andrew Lang, *The Making of Religion*, Wilhelm Schmidt, or more recently, Win Corduan, *In the Beginning, God: A Fresh Look at the Case for Original Monotheism*. Also mentioned in this chapter are G. K. Chesterton's brilliant *Everlasting Man* (*Orthodoxy* is also relevant); Gavin D'Costa, including *Theology and Religious Pluralism: The Challenge of Other Religions;* John Hick, whose thinking evolved from *God and the universe of faiths* (1973) *to A Christian Theology of Religions* (1995); Paul Radin, *Monotheism Among Primitive Peoples*; Rodney Stark, *The Discovery of God*; and James Thrower, *Religion: The Classical Theories*. On the Brothers Grimm, see G. Ronald Murphy's fascinating *The Owl, The Raven, and the Dove: The Religious Meaning of the Grimm's Magic Fairy Tales*.

Yuan Zhiming's essay, "Amazing Grace for China," which he wrote in Chinese for my anthology *Faith Seeking Understanding*, is cited in this chapter. (My translation.) I also strongly recommend his books *Lao Zi Vs. Jesus*, and *China's Confession*.

ELEVEN

Canceling Aslan

Scene: A stage rises between lawn and basketball court in Cal Anderson Park, Capitol Hill Autonomous Zone (CHAZ), with downtown Seattle skyscrapers towering in the distance. Graffiti covers a wall behind the court: "Blue Lives Murder," "BLM," "Change is in the Wind," "Shoot the Police." A tent city peeks out from under elm trees on the south edge of the park. Crowds gather as the sun sets over Puget Sound. Books are piled around a crackling bonfire with signs marked "Seuss," "Disney," "White Chick Lit," "Good Night, Moon," and "Narnia," with a large stuffed lion standing guard atop the latter pile. A man wearing a t-shirt with the legend, "Drunk Lives Matter!" leads a donkey through the crowd.

Act I: Women

Robin DiAngelo: "So you admit, Mr. Geisel, that you have no right to call yourself 'Dr.?' You appropriated medical qualifications just to elevate book sales?"

Geisel: "Well, Dartmouth did confer an honorary...."

DiAngelo: "A clear case of Zionist Privilege. Toss *Cat in the Hat* on the fire! Next!"

Bailiff: "The People vs. Aslan."

Ibram Kendi: "Who represents the author?"

Bailiff: "One Dr. Kirke. I can't find him on Facebook or Twitter. Perhaps he was banned as a white supremacist. No clue if the doctorate is genuine."

Kendi: "Jo, wanna go first?"

JK Rowling (frowning): "Neil said book-signing, not book-burning!"

Crowd: "Transphobes are mudbloods! Transphobes are mudbloods!" The chant flickers like a hint of blue flame across a damp log, then dies down. The defense advocate, an elderly man with a white beard, picks a book off the "chick lit" pile and examines the back cover.

Rowling (sighing): "All right. I'll toss out a few questions, if you don't mind, Dr. Kirke."

Kirke (looking up): "What? Oh, certainly!"

Rowling: "As you know, our age has come to see things in a different light from Lewis' era of strict gender roles. We are deeply concerned with social justice and with fair treatment of marginalized peoples, especially women and People of Color."

Kirke: "Justice is an eternal truth. And what justice cannot be social? Man has rightly been defined as a political animal."

Rowling: "That's just it, don't you see? You say 'man,' to represent all men, women, and those who feel…constricted by traditional identities. I am sure your client's stories were fine for his day. I read some of them myself, as a girl. But surely you see that times have changed? What was fitting when most women stayed home, Britain kept 'dark people' discretely in the colonies, and frankly African-Americans were treated appallingly here in the States, has often come to seem hateful and regressive."

Kirke: "The search for justice is eternal. But it is true that every age has its blind spots. That is why I have come."

Phillip Pullman: "Your bloke despised women, didn't he?"

Kirke: "Pardon me?"

Pullman: "I said, Professor Lewis did not care for women or sexuality, at least when he wrote the Narnia books. He was appalled at the notion of growing up. He favored the Ugly Sisters over Cinderella, you might say."

Kirke: "I assure you, there was nothing 'ugly' about Lucy Pevensee."

Pullman: "Don't be cute. Ms. Rowling is correct, western civilization has a horrendous record of suppressing women and minorities! And while it no doubt created great art and whatnot, in its day, the Church, 'Dr. Kirke,' was deeply complicit! Your man posed as an apologist for that faith, and used the Narnia books to brainwash children in its anti-human ideology!"

Kendi: "Hold on! That's a lot to chew on. Let's start with the charges about women, then how Lewis treated black and brown bodies. We'll get to that brainwashing business later, if the rain holds off."

Kirke: "You maintain that Professor Lewis disliked women?"

Rowling: "Sorry, Dr. Kirke, but it does sometimes come across that way. Here: 'Oh, Susan!'...'She's most interested in nothing nowadays except nylons and lipstick and invitations. She always was a jolly sight too keen on being grown-up.'"

Pullman: "Bertrand Russell called the Christian attitude towards sex 'morbid and unnatural,' and said members of Christian communities were 'diseased nervously' thanks to the dogma of their faith. I have to say Lewis' treatment of Susan confirms that diagnosis. Indeed, the whole cycle is awash with misogyny, racism, and a sado-masochistic relish for violence. A. N. Wilson suggested the sado-masochism might come from his mother. The hatred of women and dark people, he borrowed from the Church, no doubt."

Kirke: "You didn't pull any punches in that book you lent me, either, Mr. Pullman." 'For all its history, (the Church) tried to suppress and control every natural impulse. And when it can't control them, it cuts them out.'"

Pullman: "Yes, and damning Susan to hell for wearing lipstick is a pretty flagrant example!"

Kirke (Turning to Rowling with a wink): "Read on, my dear! What does Polly say in response?"

DiAngelo: "Mr. Kirke. The court suggests that you avoid patronizing and implicitly demeaning language, also sexist micro-aggressions, if you wish to persuade the Peoples' Jury. Go ahead, Ms. Rowling."

Rowling: "Thank you. 'Grown up, indeed! I wish she would grow up. She wasted all her school time wanting to be the age she is now, and she'll waste all the rest of her life trying to stay that age. Her whole idea is to race on to the silliest time of one's life as quick as she can and then stop there as long as she can.'"

Kirke: "You see, Susan's mistake was her anti-feminism, if you will: she narrowed her horizons, her conception of what it means to be human…The very mistake this tribunal is committing, I might add, by burning books."

Pullman: "But is it not clear that in Narnia, boys are better than girls?"

Kirke: "You mean, apart from Lucy, who knows Aslan better than anyone? Polly, who is consistently wise and kind-hearted? Aravis, the gutsy immigrant who helps save Narnia? Or Susan, who beats the Dwarf Trumpkin in a sharpshooting contest?"

Pullman: "Susan, you mean, tossed to the flames for liking boys? This is why the world has had enough of your 'Kingdom of Heaven,' frankly, and need the 'Republic of Heaven' I advocate. How is it healthy to expose children to this pathological fear of sexuality? Not like my Lyra. Lewis holes up with his brother, never marries, holds adolescent stag sessions with friends at the Bird and Baby...Kathy Nott nailed him in *The Observer*: 'There is little doubt that Mr. Lewis has a hankering after a return to *purdah*.'"

Kirke: "Professor Lewis has a published correspondence of more than 3000 pages. Take a peek some time, Mr. Pullman. Many letters were to women, often to those he was helping in some way. But read his letters with poets and writers—Janet Spens, Ruth Pitter, Dorothy Sayers, Sister Penelope, Evelyn Underhill, Joy Gresham, the actress Jill Flewett. They are awash with affection, playful wit, mutual respect. For a real kick in the pants, try his correspondence with a brilliant young Welsh classicist named Nan Dunbar."

Pullman: "'I have a woman friend' is your defense, is it? And his affair with Mrs. Moore?"

Kendi (holding up his hand): "Hold on! The goal of this forum is to decide what books children should avoid. We don't need the man's whole biography!"

Pullman: "Let me put it this way. When Jo and I write books for children—and the public clearly recognizes the value of those books—we are not afraid to let children of both genders grow up. But your man was traumatized by his failure to rationally defend his faith. Tossing Susan into hell is symptomatic of Lewis' diseased mind, and frankly of his religion."

The professor looked around the park. CHAZ was located in Seattle's gay district, and couples belonging to that community were well-represented, along with bodily ornaments including tattoos, rings, beads, and green or pink hair. Tourists could also be spotted, and one or two mothers with strollers. Here and there stood more militant-looking figures in black. It was a young, restless crowd, like a party in a Mad Max film, which Kirke had scanned when the landscape grew tedious over Manitoba.

Kirke: "May I be frank?"

Kendi: "It is your neck."

Kirke: "This city needs fewer riots, and more Aslan. Read Narnia through this summer, put your bricks away, and join Mr. Tumnus in the mid-summer dance.

"Mr. Pullman, you mentioned Lord Russell. The 'open' sexuality he embraced ran like a tornado through his career, wrecking every life it touched. By contrast, while the unregenerate young Lewis was a snob with a taste for sadism, every woman who knew him in later years grew richer by the acquaintance. The practice of obedience and discipline—what you call 'suppressing and controlling natural impulses'—helped make him a generous and kindly man."

Kendi: "What is this, Focus on the Family? Let's focus on literature, all right?"

Kirke: "Can we separate the two? I read your 'How to be an Anti-Racist' in a coffee shop in Oxford, Dr. Kendi. You say your parents forced you to study, and that's how you got ahead. Tell the men sleeping in those tents, destitute but for their dogs and addictions! Or the men cruising that park up on the hill at night for furtive thrills! Don't you wish these broken and lonely young men the same discipline that led to your success? Anyway, the Narnia stories were written for younger children than those of Mr. Pullman or Ms. Rowling. What is appropriate for a child of sixteen, is not even interesting to a child of nine."

Pullman: "It is presumptuous to assume we know what children will understand. Children are not monkeys climbing a stick, one notch at a time. The Christianity that Lewis and Dr. Kirke espouse cuts children off from natural feelings, from enjoying the only real world that there is!"

Kirke: "Then tell me. Almost no one goes to church on this hill, or in the UK, anymore. Your image in *The Golden Compass* of the bodies and souls of children being severed by a guillotine is brilliant. But what guillotine tears children of this unchurched generation apart? Why are there no kids playing football on this lawn? We're here to talk about children's literature. Doesn't that require readers as well as books?"

DiAngelo: "Are you offering a passive-aggressive attack on a woman's right to choose?"

Kirke: "Now that you mention it, it is odd that a supporter of unlimited abortion would warn about a guillotine that chops children in two. But I am also thinking about the consequences of encouraging twelve-year-olds to explore their sexuality, as Mr. Pullman seems to in his fiction."

Rowling (glancing at Kendi, who was scowling): "A lot of work for Mom—though I was older! But back to Lewis' regressive writings. Do you deny that reading Narnia is harmful to the self-esteem of young women?"

Kirke: "Well, first you need young women to have self-esteem, and your generation raises more dogs than children. But one can have too much self-esteem. Listen to what they wrote on the back of this modern printing of one of my old favorites: 'For today's reader *Jane Eyre* is above all, the story of a woman of passion and intelligence who refuses to be satisfied with her 'place' in society, and asserts her identity and aspirations with defiance and dignity.'"

DiAngelo: "Do you object to women being treated with dignity?"

Kirke: "What I object to is the self-praise this generation bathes in, as in a tub full of lard! Do you really suppose that a literature that produced Queen Esther, the *Song of Songs*, the Wife of Bath, Emma, and the heroines of Middlemarch, needs to be chewed up into 'moral cliff notes' and made digestible to young minds? We should protect sensitive self-'identities,' while ignoring the forces that rip young lives to shreds, set young men begging on the streets for their next fix, and young women to cutting off their own breasts like Amazons, or forced to go on the dole and raise children by themselves?"

Pullman: "'I do not permit women to speak in the churches.' Shouldn't young women be protected from Taliban-like thinking of that sort?"

Kirke (glaring): "Has anyone told you, Mr. Pullman, that it is wrong to tell lies?"

Pullman: "I'm quoting directly from your own sacred Scriptures."

Kirke: "But why pick that verse, out of hundreds? Why not verses that show women leading armies, buying and selling real estate, taking the initiative in love, speaking for God, or saving their cities or nations?"

Pullman: "The issue is the trauma your man inflicts on young women by making them feel guilty for exploring their sexual nature! You want to turn this discussion into anything but what it is: a needed rebuke to the cruelty of the man you neglect to defend!"

Kirke frowned, took matches from his pocket, and lit a pipe. The fumes joined with smoke from the books and marijuana haze, creating an aromatic smog that drifted south towards a boarded-up police station.

Kirke: "Susan grew fearful of love. And that, I fear, as Aslan put it, is a warning to your world."

Pullman: "I may not believe in God, but I do know that a woman's right to choose is sacred." (Cheers.)

Kirke (sighing): "What do they teach them in these schools? If choice is free, how can some choices not be wrong? Austen, Eliot, and the Bronte sisters created worlds in which a woman's choice meant something: an affair, a grudge, a spiteful visit to your nephew's lover, a wrong choice in lovers, all bore consequences. But 'celebrating choice' without considering whether those choices lead to heaven or hell, infantilizes women, in the name of liberating them."

DiAngelo: "In Christendom, women were treated as baby machines. Intentionally or not, that is the bourgeois, cis-gendered ideology that Narnia perpetuates."

Kirke: "I admit that history is complex."

DiAngelo: "Thank you!"

Kirke: "And it is true that some Christian thinkers who ought to have known better, seemed to fear or dislike women."

DiAngelo: "Thanks again! Well that's putting it mildly!"

Kirke: "But C. S. Lewis was not one of them. And no one has liberated women around the world more than Jesus of Nazareth."

The man on the donkey handed DiAngelo a goblet, and she swallowed its contents in one gulp.

DiAngelo: "You have got to be kidding. Can you back that up in any way whatsoever?"

Kirke: "In many ways. First, the United Nations examined the status of women around the world by health, economics, family life, social equality, and employment. The twenty countries with the highest rankings all shared a Christian heritage."

DiAngelo: "So according to your male perspective, the fact that Christians denied the priesthood, the vote, even inheritance, to European women is no big deal? The Church should get credit because the Enlightenment began to liberate women from the shackles in which it had for so long placed them, as Simone De Beauvoir has shown?"

Kirke: "Jesus liberated women from the beginning. That's why most early Christians were female. Enlightenment thinkers? Rousseau and Shelley were sexual predators. De Beauvoir lost her teaching position because she had a habit of seducing students, then passing them on to her boyfriend, the philosopher Jean-Paul Sartre."

Cat-calls came from several directions. The old man slowly made his way around the podium to the front of the stage, almost slipping on a grape vine that had mysteriously sprung up.

Kirke: "You came tonight, because you know that life is more than lipstick or dates. It never dawned on Alexander the Great or Julius Caesar that 'non-elite lives matter.' You got that from Aslan. In a sense, you are his children. But meaning no disrespect to Ms. De Beauvoir, or our friend Ms. DiAngelo, you have been seduced by a White Witch."

Crowd: "Our bodies our choice!"

Kirke: "Choice? Little girls in the ancient world were often abandoned at birth, or fed to brothels. Followers of Jesus took those girls in, and let them marry later than pagans. Muslim visitors to Medieval Europe expressed amazement at the liberty women had."

Pullman: "So Hwin and stay-at-home Mrs. Beaver with her Singer sowing machine are the truest feminist heroes, in your light?"

Rowling: "I think I get Kirke's point. Zoologists say that if you destroy a family of elephants, the survivors become miserable and misbehave. Society has become a lonely place for far too many young people. Up in the Midlands, thousands of girls were abused by Paki grooming gangs, and police and parents lacked the balls to protect them. Or they were just absent. But surely you don't wish to drag women back to the Middle Ages, do you, Mr. Kirke?"

Kirke: "Neither Lewis, nor his Savior, even limited women to the home, like Penelope waiting in the women's quarters for Odysseus to return. Mrs. Beaver, Aravis, and Hwin helped save Narnia. And if you want real-world heroines, read how missionaries like Gladys Aylward shamed villagers in Shanxi to stop breaking the bones of young girls, then led orphans across the mountains of northern China past Japanese Zeros. Or how Amy Carmichael and Pandita Ramabai saved girls from brothels in India. Learn how Mary Slessor rebuked African patriarchs on behalf of girls who had no other protector. Or Jackie Pullinger, pulling drug-addicted gangsters out of the Walled City in Hong Kong by their ears, and praying them off drugs. New Testament scholar Walter Wink argues that Jesus challenged gender conventions in every single meeting with women. From him flows the liberation that CHAZ, Afghanistan, and Yorkshire all need.

"Nothing but smoke comes from burning books. Study them instead! No one has done more to elevate women than Jesus of Nazareth. You need people like Lewis, who follow him, and open their hearts wholeheartedly to women, and men, in need."

Kendi (rapping a gavel): "While Lewis' sexual peccadillos may be interesting, and these pseudo-historical jeremiads worth debating some other day, let's focus on the true problem with Lewis: race. And when I say 'focus,' Dr. Kirke, I do mean focus. The man really had it in for colored people, right? Maybe that would be a stronger basis for canceling Aslan."

Act II: Racism

Kendi: "Didn't your man Plato warn against telling immoral stories to children? Here we have a book—I grew up in the church, you know—let's see: 'Two merchants of Calormen at once approached. The Calormen have DARK faces and long beards. They wear flowing robes and orange-colored turbans, and they are a wise, wealthy, courteous, CRUEL and ancient people.'"

"The pagans in Narnia are colored! Even the slave-traders are black! How's that for projection? And these people with dark skin worship a devil bird, then invade Narnia! Who are good, clean, god-fearing white folk. This seems like a pretty instance of poisoning children's minds with racism, if not white supremacy!"

Pullman: "Absolutely true, Dr. Kendi! And the bad dwarves are 'black' while the good dwarves are 'red.' Society can no longer tolerate such blatant racism! And in *The Last Battle*, that won your man the Carnegie Medal, Kirke, the heroes rub on a juice that makes them 'brown as Calormenes.' When they take off their disguises, King Tirian says, let's see, here it is: "'Body of me! That is better. I feel a true man again!'"

Crowd: "Aslan is a Racist!" (A brick breaks on stage.)

Kendi (kicking a fragment to one side): "Not cool! Is that you, Smurf? Can someone from the John Brown Rifle Club please escort this hothead out? Thank you. We're just having a friendly conversation about the fate of Western Civilization. (Scattered laughter.)

"Is it not true that in addition to these blatantly racist statements about brown bodies and black bodies being less worthy than white bodies, that your client, Mr. Clives Staples Lewis, almost totally ignored non-white literature?"

Kirke: "Is literature the name of a color?"

Pullman: "Well, it seems that in Lewis' view, only light-colored people wrote anything worth reading!"

Kirke: "Actually, Lewis often fantasized about learning Persian, the likely model for Calormen, because he thought he was missing out on lots of great poetry. But yes, Lewis and Tolkien wrote when Britain was almost entirely English-speaking and white. No doubt if they wrote in 2022, their stories would reflect the ethnic diversity of modern Oxford. But their minds were steeped in the consciousness of Medieval Europe, which had for centuries been surrounded south, east and even west (in Spain) by powerful Islamic armies which tried to conquer Europe.

Crowd: "Islamophobe! Islamophobe!"

Kendi: "There you go!"

Kirke: "And as a young man, Lewis was rather bigoted, as you say you once were, Dr. Kendi—against white Americans. During the Second World War, he noted with satisfaction that black GIs seemed more welcome in the UK. He often made rude remarks about Americans in his early letters. That bias took a while to grow out of, though he eventually found himself with many close American friends."

Kendi: "So you're saying that Lewis was actually anti-racist?"

Kirke: "No, I am saying you need to escape from the ideological stable in which you've trapped yourselves. I notice CHAZ only allows African-Americans to play on this court during daylight hours. Isn't that what you used to mean by racism? And isn't racism just one prejudice, and prejudice one of many tools by which the White Witch binds people to the Stone Table?"

Kendi: "You forget who's on trial, here, professor. How do you explain the instances of racism we demonstrated?"

Kirke: "By asking you to read the books more carefully. Aravis the Calormene was proud and a touch cruel, growing up in a ruthless empire. But she was also brave, romantic, faithful to friends (even if she didn't like them), and a skilled story-teller. She was welcomed as a daughter by the king of Archenland, and ended up marrying the male lead. That's racism? That's misogyny? Plato taught us the importance of justice. And Jesus showed us to care for those on the margins. But William Blake has something to teach this generation, too: 'The iron hand crushed the Tyrant's head / And became a tyrant in his stead.' "Red Guards should beware of becoming the evil that they hate."

DiAngelo: "Let's not blind ourselves to the reality. Look at the faces of tech CEOs! White males still hold the real power in western civilization! The revolution has a long ways to go!"

Rowling: "Yet we four are among the most powerful people in the world!"

DiAngelo: "As a social scientist, I look at the aggregate, Ms. Rowling. I suggest you look beyond your own bank account."

Rowling: "Fine. Call me mud-blood, if you like. But, to be honest, Harry Potter does not tell the whole story. In Harry, you have Death Eaters on one side, and the Order of the Phoenix on the other, nice and clean, good versus evil. The bad lot wind up as death-eaters, while the good 'uns join Harry and fight for all that is holy. But life is not so simple, is it?

"Call it 'intermediate power.' Everyone has it: a baby over her bowels, a teacher over his students, a mob with bricks and water bottles, or the kitchen help who can spit in your soup if they like. Power is always in flux, and dualities flip, like magnetic poles. The real Death Eater, I have come to see, is the one who treats oppression or virtue as a constant, or externalizes evil into some fixed group—whatever that group is. Virtue has no fixed residence."

Kirke: "Lewis said something very like that in the *Abolition of Man*."

DiAngelo: "'Man,' again. Presumably he meant women and men?"

Kendi: "Look, Dr. Kirke. I don't hate religion. I grew up Christian, and quote the Bible sometimes, like when it says that humans are one at heart. But what do philosophical jeremiads have to do with children's education?"

Kirke: "Actually, *Abolition of Man* (women and men, if you prefer) is precisely about what books children should read. The core concept of the book is the Chinese term 'Tao,' from Confucius. 'Tao' was an all-pervading truth underlying creation itself—'deeper magic,' one might say. It the ultimate moral truth that everyone finds written on their hearts. Teaching the Tao means building a rational foundation for justice in the hearts of students."

Pullman: "Professor, this is a tribunal. We are deciding whether or not to allow children to read books which carry patently racist sentiments, arising in a deeply racist Christian civilization. Please do not waste our time."

Kirke: "Here's the narrow point. Note the sources Lewis cites for universal moral truth: 'Ancient Egyptian;' 'Ancient Jewish;' 'the Near East;' 'Old Norse;' 'Babylonian;' 'Hindu;' 'Ancient Chinese;' 'Roman;' 'Redskin' (he meant 'Native American;') 'Greek;' 'Australian Aboriginies;' 'Anglo-Saxon;' 'Christian.' Lewis didn't care about anything so trivial as skin color. His point was that people around the world recognize a broad set of moral truths: mercy, magnanimity, justice, good faith, benevolence, duties to children and posterity, duties to the old and infirm."

Kendi: "Traditional values? Like justifying the enslavement of my people?"

Kirke: "We are holding this trial in what may be the only city in the world named for two slave-owners: Chief Seattle, and

George Washington. How did attitudes about slavery begin to change?"

Kendi: "Jesus, I suppose?"

Kirke: "You smile, but historians know he led the fight. Slavery began to fade in Medieval Europe under theological pressure—but not in Islam, Africa, or India. The Portuguese revived commercial slavery as European states competed to rule the world. But Quakers and 'Clapham' evangelicals challenged that ancient custom theologically. The British government not only made slavery illegal, and twisted the arms of the French to do the same, but started sending out war ships to liberate slaves of other nations. The Dawn Treader can be seen as the last of that fleet, carrying the evangelical policies of Her Majesty's Government to the Lone Islands."

Kendi: "Are you trying to give Lewis credit for praising policies enacted a century before his time?"

Kirke: "Not Lewis. Aslan. But tell me, Dr. Kendi. Why is racism wrong?"

Kendi: "Why what?"

Kirke: "I'm not challenging that it is wrong. I'm asking you, as a professor of anti-racist studies, to explain the error of racism from first principles!"

Kendi: "OK, I'll bite. Genetic diversity among humans is minute compared to that among other hominids. Ethnicities, therefore, should not be set into an artificial hierarchy ... Racism is a form of bigotry, a failure to treat other people with due respect."

Kirke: "'Black Lives Matter,' you say. The other day, Horace Lorenzo died a few paces from this stand. Did his life matter as much as that of George Floyd? Nine out of ten murders in America are of people of one race, killing other people of the same race. Nearly all murders are of people of one gender, killing others of the same gender. Shouldn't we also care about lives that do not fit into the present 'social justice' narrative? Isn't murder, by definition, the ultimate abuse of power?"

A hush fell over the audience, not of quiet inebriation, still less boredom. It was the fragile quiet of a jury hearing the defendant openly confess his guilt, and watch in shocked fascination as he leans forward and bares his neck for the noose.

"Hate has no place here!" Yelled a middle-aged woman in short pink hair, lobbing a cluster of grapes that struck Kirke in chest.

DiAngelo: "Hold that thought a bit longer, folks! Let's see how Lewis treated educational progressives, first. Pullman, end this fiasco."

Act III: Education

Pullman: "Christians talk a lot about love. But Lewis demeaned progressives and those who stand up against fascism! At the end of *The Silver Chair*, Lewis takes loathsome glee in describing how children from a progressive school are beaten. I quote directly, so Kirke need not question my integrity this time:

> Suddenly they stopped. Their faces changed, and all the meanness, conceit, cruelty, and sneakishness almost disappeared in one single expression of terror. For they saw the wall fallen down, and a lion as large as a young elephant lying in the gap, and three figures in glittering clothes with weapons in their hands rushing down upon them. For, with the strength of Aslan in them, Jill plied her crop on the girls and Caspian and Eustace plied the

flats of their swords on the boys so well that in two minutes all the bullies were running like mad, crying out, 'Murder! Fascists! Lions! It isn't fair.'"

Crowd: "Boo!" More grapes rained onto the stage.

Pullman: "The POLICE investigated and people got expelled, no doubt People of Color."

Crowd: "Blue Lives Murder! Blue Lives Murder!"

Pullman: "I detest the supernaturalism, the reactionary sneering, the misogyny, the racism, and the sheer dishonesty of Lewis' stories. But even I find this shocking. This man here is standing up for fascism, beating school children, and sneering at progressives!"

Kirke (wiping grape juice off his cheek, mixed with blood where a rock had glancingly struck below his right eye): "Actually, the woman complaining about fascism was protecting youths who tortured small children. Mrs. Rowling referred to intermediate powers. With due respect, Mr. Pullman, if you don't see the good of teaching bullies to fear God, you have no business writing for youth. And see what happened to those bullies: Their faces changed, and all the meanness, conceit, cruelty, and sneakiness almost disappeared in one single expression of terror.' In other words, fear began to reinstate their lost humanity."

"Lewis once wrote about a 'Mr. Savage,' who drank wine from human skulls. Savage's disciples were Communists and Nazis alike. In *Mein Kampf*, Adolf Hitler tells how he learned the value of terror from Marxist construction workers in Vienna who tried to throw him off the scaffolding. 'Fascists' and 'anti-fascists' copy one another: 'memetic rivalry,' it has been called. Both seek power by bullying and dehumanizing the weak. Beware of becoming what you hate."

DiAngelo: "So when you look at Women of Color standing up for justice, you see Nazis?"

Kirke: "I see broken saints. I see Moses, bringing a shattered table of law down from Mount Sinai. I see King David, building Jerusalem on cracked foundations. I see St. Paul spreading a Gospel that could fit on a fortune cookie. I see God Himself, creating novel genders for a New Heaven and Earth made from an acorn. I see children playing hide-and-seek in my house in the country, having left their souls like jackets back in Charn.

"What forlorn deities you have become! This nation of CHAZ, founded in one of the richest and most beautiful cities in the world, has a higher murder rate than Guatemala. It is covered with graffiti and begins to stink. You tear down statues, not because the men or women they depict were racists, but because you fear Aslan will breathe on them, and they will come to life. You closed the wardrobe door, and are lost among moth balls."

Crowd: "Cancel! Cancel! Cancel!"

The mob began to surge towards the stage, throwing Lewis' books on the fire. Professor Kirke put a hand in his pocket and disappeared. J. K. Rowling messaged her fellow judges that she had left for a meeting in Cleveland. A copy of Abolition of Man disappeared with her.

The next day, city sanitation workers of multiple races and genders came to cart trash away. They found the stuffed lion in the tent of a homeless man. It had been thrown into the fire along with three copies of the Abolition of Man, but the books and lion all mysteriously came out unsinged.

TWELVE

Imagining Truth

"He thought of course that [Lucy and Edmund) were making [Narnia) up; and as he was far too stupid to make up anything himself, he did not approve of that." Voyage of the Dawn Treader

On an ocean planet in a fictional version of our solar system, a traveler discovered two kinds of land forms. First, after swimming in a sea of mountainous waves until exhausted, he dragged himself up onto masses of flexible vegetable matter that rose and fell on the surface. Those matted islands drifted apart or merged to form a little continent. On them, beneath an orange, silver, and blue canopy, tube-trees produced shimmering bubbles, and fruits grew whose scent was so delectable that it "created a new kind of hunger and thirst."

Later the traveler found his way from this floating paradise to more solid land, where reddish mountains soared above the sea. As the wind passed over highland trees less than waist high, navy-blue streamers floated from their boughs, making the land seem to flow like water. Mountain mice ran beneath this shimmering foliage.

Clive Staples Lewis was a man of the archipelago. He created a vast flotilla of literary works, like islands that drift together, allowing a visitor to jump from one to another. Lewis' eclectic tastes formed early. His brother dreamt up an imaginary India, he created Animal Land, then they merged these lands into the nation of

"Boxen." Meetings of the Inklings, the club Jack Lewis formed at Oxford, also ranged widely, joined by filaments of laughter, mockery, piety, and beer: medicine, philosophy, a chapter from Warnie on France, a chapter from "Tullers" on "the new Hobbit." Lewis' literary creations sometimes scattered, sometimes bunched, driven on currents of whimsy and insight.

John Ronald Reuel Tolkien, by contrast, was a patriotic inhabitant of a Fixed Land, more Farmer Maggot or Treebeard than some wandering wizard. He spent most of his life laying the foundations of Middle Earth, inventing languages, mapping history and mythologies, describing the adventures of its heroes. Lewis loved his friend's Fixed Land, visited often, and encouraged its construction. Sometimes Tolkien visited Lewis' archipelago, too, but seemed to quickly get homesick for his own, more rooted territory.

Plato was right: the stories we hear as youths form us. Mom read me and my siblings *Heidi, Where the Read Fern Grows,* and *The Jungle Book.* Dad, a Calvinist, recounted Christian's adventures seeking the Celestial City. How happy I was when a teacher lent me a pass to visit the wooden library upstairs, and search shelves for books about Christopher Robin and friends.

Then I discovered Lewis and Tolkien. Winnie the Pooh would always remain a bear of small brain, but Aslan and Gandalf grew with me. What I gained from Tolkien directly mostly came from the Fixed Land he constructed. (Along with "Leaf, by Niggle," "On Fairy Stories," and a view from the summit of other islands in the chain of Nordic myth, like *Beowulf* and the *Poetic Edda.*) Lewis introduced me to a more scattered archipelago: Boswell, Chesterton, Eyre, Haggard, Holst, MacDonald, Milton, Scott, Stephens, Virgil, Wagner, Wordsworth, Yeats. My literary world also became "dappled," as Gerard Hopkins put it, a "landscape plotted and pieced" with sources, ideas, even habits of life drawn from Lewis' work. For instance, after he met Aslan on the mountain pass, the hungry Shasta learned a new way of eating breakfast, which he taught me:

> Immediately, mixed with a sizzling sound, there came to Shasta a simply delightful smell. It was one he had never smelt in his life before, but I hope you have. It was, in fact, the smell of bacon and eggs and mushrooms all frying in a pan.

A high school student by now, I had started cooking breakfast for myself. Reading that, I sliced up mushrooms and sautéed them in butter with my eggs and bacon. Farmer Maggot could have taught me to love mushrooms, but Tolkien didn't say how hobbits cooked them!

The ocean on which Lewis' thin islands float is truth as he saw it. Chesterton argued that the Gospel unites those who seek truth, with those who tell stories:

> It met the mythological search for romance by being a story and the philosophical search for truth by being a true story. That is why the ideal figure had to be a historical character as nobody had ever felt Adonis or Pan to be a historical character. But that is also why the historical character had to be the ideal figure; and even fulfill many of the functions given to these other ideal figures; why he was at once the sacrifice and the feast.

Why, in his fifties, did the world's foremost defender of the Christian faith begin writing for kids? Like Professor Kirke, he had welcomed children to his rural home during the Blitz. Talking with those urchins likely helped him find the right voice. But it does seem odd that an aging professor with no children, who mostly avoided other children when he was young himself, would suddenly dash off a fantasy series in rug-rat level language.

(Yet laced with weighty philosophy.) Can classics really be a sign of cowardice?

Surely A. N. Wilson was wrong about that. For one thing, many of Lewis' best apologetic pieces were written after his famous debate with Elizabeth Anscombe, including "Fernseed and Elephants." Four years into Narnia, Oxford Press published his magisterial *Poetry and Prose in the 16th Century*. After Narnia, Lewis also wrote ground-breaking academic works for Cambridge U Press: *Study in Words*, *Experiment in Criticism*, and *The Discarded Image*. He nursed a truly great novel out of the myth of Eros and Psyche. His step-son Douglas asked (he said in a letter in 1960), "When are you going to stop writing all that bilge and write interesting books again?" In fact, he was busy writing "bilge" of profound genius. He told children he had finished with Narnia, inviting them to try writing their own sequels.

Tolkien came to feel that in *The Hobbit*, he had sometimes talked down to children too much. In a letter to his aunt, Jane Neave, he wrote: "I am not interested in the 'child' as such, modern or otherwise, and certainly have no intention of meeting him / her half way, or a quarter of the way."

Lord of the Rings was written "for itself." If children landed on Tolkien's island, they should not expect to conquer its peaks, though they were welcome to gather samples from its rich mine of vocabulary. More than Tolkien, Lewis met audiences halfway, and did write for children, when he felt like it, as well as for himself and the "work itself."

Lewis said that children's stories were the right genre to say certain things. A fawn carrying presents through snowy woods had come to mind. He was "with book," he also explained (and lent this metaphor to his heroine in *Till We Have Faces*.)

Dwight Longenecker preferred Tolkien's fixed land:

Tolkien took myth more seriously. He built his alternative world from the ground up. Beginning with the language of the elves, Tolkien created the race that spoke the language, then conceived and carefully created not only the other races and their languages, but the whole world in which they lived, complete with its geography, history, and comprehensive myth. Tolkien may have been scornful of the rapidity and ease with which Lewis created his stories, but he was so not simply because the works were produced quickly, but because it showed.

Tolkien found Narnia a "mishmash" of poorly-connected elements: classical myths, modern folklore, children's literature. What has Bacchus to do with Beatrix Potter?

True, Lewis' stories sometimes got overloaded. *That Hideous Strength* gives us school politics, a totalitarian dystopia, a bear, a tramp, a cigar-chewing lesbian Gestapo head, angels from outer space, and Merlin the Magician. Lewis even mentions Tolkien's mythology, to his friend's chagrin.

Like animals pouring into Noah's Ark, creatures flood onto the floating islands of imagination called Narnia, too. We meet centaurs, satyrs, and gods from Greece. Dwarves pour over the border from the *Edda*, the Norse classic which Lewis, Tolkien, and friends read together. We meet children like those Jack and Warnie took in during the Blitzkrieg, perverse school administrators (though none as cruel as Robert Capron under whom the Lewis brothers suffered), and a professor who might have been Lewis himself.

But this reflects a conscious literary philosophy, developed in light of Lewis' deep reading. Did not Dante, Spenser, and Apuleius mix elements as well? Tolkien's beloved *Beowulf* combines Christian faith with pagan monsters. *Journey to the West*, treasured by generations of Chinese, likewise joins Buddhist philosophy, kung fu, slap-stick, and Tang court concerns, and echoes the *Clas-*

sic of Mountains and Seas in placing monsters on every peak on the way to India. The Bible itself is a remarkably eclectic anthology.

One might call Tolkien a hedgehog, and Lewis a fox, to use Isaiah Berlin's categories. Tolkien dug deep in one spot. Lewis jumped from rock to rock, ever curious, in that sense more "catholic" than his friend. Lucy found Aslan on every island where the Dawn Treader landed.

Both were philosophers whose veins ran with the blood of elves. By mapping truth across islands of imagination, fixed and floating, they also mapped it across our world.

I will gladly follow Gandalf through Middle Earth, by dragons and balrogs, and up mountains chased by ring wraiths. But never past the doors that lead into Narnia. (Even if one does find errors, such as the White Witch telling Edmund the way back to England, when she obviously had no clue a few minutes before.)

For Lewis' ability to integrate worlds was part of his insight. His spirit was the opposite of that of Cancel Culture: he loved every wind, frost, and squall, of words or atmosphere. Lewis treasured Percy Shelley, Bertrand Russell's "Worship of a Free Man," David Lindsay, and HG Wells, and carried on hilarious correspondence with E. R. Eddison in Old English, while vehemently disagreeing with their atheistic or even "diabolical" airs.

Far from retreating from the adult world to write Narnia, Lewis tasted the best fruits on each tree of fancy and fact. He thus offered reasons for Christian faith that enlarge the islands of our imagination, and situated them in the ultimate Fixed Land of Truth.

Doors into Narnia

I left my own Shire of West Seattle, and plunged into a sea of opposing faiths at university, then in Asia. Sometimes I seemed to catch the voice of "Aslan" in the Utter East. But I also heard the raucous cry of Tash, nesting among sex slaves in Snake Alley, rising from the blood-stained Forbidden City, shrieking over its prey as Sikhs and Hindus came to blows in New Delhi after the killing of Indira Gandhi. As Chesterton did for him, Lewis helped me see how Christ unites and fulfills the human story, joining truths at their deepest roots, challenging falsehoods and setting captives free. Because these, too, are Aslan's lands, fixed or floating.

The White Witch and her minions were chasing Peter and his gang when they met a party of squirrels, dwarves, satyrs, and a fox, eating a plum pudding. Jadis demanded they explain "this gluttony, this waste, this self-indulgence." When a frightened young squirrel insisted it was all a gift from Father Christmas, she turned them all into stone. And Edmund, "for the first time in this story, felt sorry for someone besides himself."

I "awoke" before Wokeness, the prophet Isaiah splashing water on my face. The White Witch had turned the hearts of tribal girls in Southeast Asia into stone, and their bodies were sold to make a buck. Meeting such women in a village in northern Thailand, I felt sorry for someone besides myself. For the second time in my life, a Voice seemed to speak to me in words clear enough to transcribe: "Just as I sent my Son into the world to save it, so I want to send my children into this tribe, this village, to die for it and give it new life."

Decades later, as principal of a new "American" school in China, I gathered books for a little library. I set Digory, Frodo, Hermione, Lyra, and Katniss Everdeen together on a prominent shelf labeled "young adult fantasy series." Volumes on that shelf quickly disappeared. A talented but contrarian student had been reading Joseph Campbell, and I guided her as she flipped his ideas and explored the "Anti-hero with a Thousand Faces." She gave herself the English name of Lyra, after the God-defeating heroine of

Phillip Pullman's books. I also created World Literature textbooks that included *Prometheus Bound* by the Greek playwright Aeschylus. Prometheus was the titan who gave gifts like medicine and fire to humanity. The king of the gods, Zeus, angrily chained him up, and an eagle came to peck his liver. Pullman's *Dark Materials* play on the same hatred of tyrants divine and mortal.

All truth is God's truth, Lewis taught me. Let students jump into many ponds. Some might become Fixed Lands of their imaginations: helping them to both "escape" from this world and to test understandings of it scientifically. Even literary images of hell often ring true: *Animal Farm, 1984, Brave New World, Fahrenheit 451, The Matrix, Uncle Tom's Cabin, The Handmaid's Tale.* At the heart of every sound dystopia lies some heresy, some worm that spoils the apple, or witch who holds it out, drenched with poison, for our destruction.

Aslan welcomed even Bacchus, the Greek god of drink, drama, and insanity, into his world. Alone, Bacchus becomes "baka," as the Japanese say: a fool. But his foolishness is also a floating island in the great Chain of Truth which C. S. Lewis explored with lifelong delight.

Bacchus in Narnia

At that moment the sun was just rising and Lucy remembered something and whispered to Susan.

"I say, Su. I know who they are."

"Who?"

"The boy with the wild face is Bacchus and the old one on the donkey is Silenus. Don't you remember Mr. Tumnus telling us about them long ago?"

"Yes, of course. But I say, Lu –"

"What?"

"I wouldn't have felt safe with Bacchus and all his wild girls if we'd met them without Aslan."

"I should think not," said Lucy.

Dionysius (Bacchus in Greek) was the god of madness, vengeance, uprooted trees, mangled deer, and a bloody form of Cancel Culture. The young Lewis attended brilliant lectures on *The Bacchantes* by Gilbert Murray at Christ Church College, and mentioned the play in letters throughout his life.

In writing Narnia, Lewis recognized the need to "get in touch with his emotions." But Bacchus also needed a Master, so that even insanity might talk sense.

The fractured insights of our Bacchian era need mastering as well. The idea that Narnia is "violent," "misogynistic," or "racist," is a stupidity worthy of this age, perhaps reflecting our fear of innocence. We need something lighter, healthier, and more balanced than the pathogens that choke these flasks. We need the *Tao*, a full moral vision, a series of islands floating lightly upon universal truths. In the kindness of the Beavers, the faith of Trufflehunter, the valiance of Reepicheep, and the insight of Puddleglum, we feel the current of the *Tao* flowing beneath our feet, and catch a whiff of paradise.

But Euripides would not be surprised at the canceling of Aslan, in Narnia or in CHAZ. Rene Girard pointed out that scapegoating frenzies often occur during epidemics. He argued that Jesus threw down a gauntlet to all bullies and lynch mobs. His death undermines scapegoating by revealing the guilt of the mob and the lameness of their excuses.

The Gifts of Father Christmas

Narnia is not just a series of gentle children's stories. Nor is it an irresponsible flight of imagination by an over-the-hill philosopher. It is a series of flasks in which ideas are tested. And we have seen that the results of those experiments ring true. Aslan's Song of Creation helps explain the origins of the cosmos. Physics proves that the universe must have begun in a highly-ordered state. Stars, hydrogen and carbon, organic molecules, prokaryotes, lungs, noses, wings, family, language, and self-awareness evoke harmonies within the fabric of Nature. Touch a stone, and it vibrates to the rhythms of creation. Great scientists transcribe formulae and recognize patterns, sometimes against their will, as notes of some grand orchestration.

Aslan's talk of "deeper magic" helps us understand what a "miracle" is, and why God's signs are in sync with science. Aslan does not "work against the Emperor's magic," the laws of creation, exclusion, cause and effect, or even the karmic principle that "the soul that sins, will surely die." Rather, miracles reveal a deeper magic that saves those trapped in the Giants' castle.

"The *Tao* was made flesh," says the Chinese Bible. Scott Peck called Jesus "wise, but weird." Gospel portraits of him could not have been drawn by any fiction-writing genius, still less by random first century fishermen or tax collectors. In Christ's gaze, the lives of those who meet him gain new meaning.

Within the petri dish of Narnia, Professor Kirke found reasons to believe Lucy's story. Dozens of powerful lines of evidence more objectively support the historicity of the gospels. To exchange one known genius for numerous unknown fabricators, would be like explaining Shakespeare by saying *MacBeth*, *Hamlet*, *Romeo and Juliet*, and *The Tempest*, were produced by random members of a ladies' knitting circle in Stratford-on-Avon.

C. S. Lewis is the Poet Laurette of weighted choice. Friends of Narnia are not sorted by a hat into schools that reflect their unchanging character. Way leads on to way, and the choices they make help reveal the significance of our choices, as well.

Drive to the end of the road half an hour north of Mendenhall Valley where I discovered Narnia. Hike along a beach festooned with seaweed, around cliffs of shale (my friends and I tried to camp in a cave in those cliffs at young teenagers, but they leaked in the rain and we burnt our tent). Round a rocky corner, and a beautiful valley opens to the southwest: miles of grass, lupine, iris, fireweed, and Alaska cotton, a river running through it to a bay surrounded by snow-capped peaks. Berners' Bay reminds me of the lake that Digory and Polly flew to on Fledge. Sweet fruit grow at Echo Ranch Bible Camp, too: wild strawberries and nagoon berries in the grass, blueberries under spruce and hemlock, past where I carried slop buckets of left-over food to leave for the bears.

Other young counselors were off somewhere one evening, and I picked up a copy of *Mere Christianity* to read by myself in the dining room. A chapter entitled "The Great Sin," about pride, shone a harsh spotlight on my life. Like Eustace, I could be pouty and withdrawn. Like Susan, I often cared more about things than people. Like Rabadash, I manipulated those around me. My heart could be winter without Christmas. I shut the door to my own stable.

Pullman is right, Lewis was cruel to the little Jadis in my heart. He is mean as grass so solid it hurts the feet to walk upon, like an apple too heavy to carry, or lion claws that cut into one's back, to heal, not to harm.

We enjoy a Golden Age of historical arguments for the Resurrection of Jesus. But we must also remember the "deeper magic." The Resurrection is credible not only because there is evidence for it, but because of Whom it happened to. We can trust the Word made flesh, because we see Him sing worlds to life: freeing prostitutes and drug addicts, founding schools and hospitals, ending infanticide and the murder of widows. Can it be coincidence that the resurrection story is told (with dozens of lines of supporting evidence) about the one Man of whom it proves most believable?

Aslan ties Narnia together, from creation to final judgment and renewal. Just so no history of sons of Adam and daughters of Eve is sound without Jesus at center. (Though that is not what they teach them in these schools.) Jesus is the bridge from "BC" to "AD," from tyranny and chaos to progress and justice, just as early humans passed through Palestine to disperse around the world. Many signs point us to the bridge of Christ, even in pagan mythology, even in post-Christian philosophy and science.

But the *Tao* is an aircraft engine from which parts have worked loose and been spit into the turbines. The Second Century Christian teacher Clement, who lived in the city of Alexandria, saw in the fate of Pentheus, the king who offended Dionysius, a metaphor for our madness:

> Truth is one…Just as the Bacchantes tore asunder the limbs of Pentheus, so the sects bboth of barbarian and Hellenic philosophy have done with truth, and each vaunts as the whole truth the portion which has fallen to its lot. But all, in my opinion, are illuminated by the dawn of Light.

One popular sect today is an offshoot of Marxism called Critical Theory. The Gospel anticipates and fulfills the important truths that give it what life and persuasive value it holds: that God will judge us on how we treat the hungry. But Christ also liberates us from the bonfire furies, self-righteousness, and hypocrisies of simplistic revolutions, and from conservative responses that merely wave the flag and blindly cheer on "the other team."

So no, Lewis did not "retreat" into Narnia from adult concerns and tough arguments. Rather, Aslan made a "petri dish" of our imagination: a cordial made of the juice of fire-flowers that grow in the sun, of blended kindness and truth, to help heal the wounds that afflict our souls.

YOU MIGHT ALSO LIKE

Mere Humanity
G.K. Chesterton, C.S. Lewis, and J.R.R. Tolkien on the Human Condition

"Is Man a Myth?" asks the title of one of Mr. Tumnus's books. It was apparently an open question in Narnia during the Long Winter, and it has become so again for us. In *Mere Humanity*, Donald T. Williams plumbs the writings of three beloved Twentieth-Century authors to find answers that still resonate in the Twenty-First. Chesterton, Lewis, and Tolkien explain in their expositions and incarnate in their fiction a robust biblical doctrine of man that gives us a firm place to stand against the various forms of reductionism that dominate our thinking about human nature today.

For a full listing of our books, visit DeWard's website:
www.deward.com